Bernadette,

Thank you for your inspiration + to your powerful commitment to our being all we've been created to be. May you know all you've blessed us with. Blessing multiplied return of

We hope you'll enjoy our daughter-in-law's latest publication. core Lilia is that we are created for, something that is expressed through love, in all you do.

Blessings & much love,
Love and Benedict

Integrating the
New Science of Love
and a
Spirituality of Peace

Integrating the
New Science of Love
and a
Spirituality of Peace

Becoming Human Again

Edited by
Christian E. Early
and
Annmarie L. Early

CASCADE *Books* · Eugene, Oregon

INTEGRATING THE NEW SCIENCE OF LOVE AND A SPIRITUALITY OF PEACE
Becoming Human Again

Cascade Books
An Imprint of Wipf and Stock Publishers
199 W. 8th Ave., Suite 3
Eugene, OR 97401

www.wipfandstock.com

ISBN 13: 978-1-62032-871-2

Cataloguing-in-Publication data:

Integrating the new science of love and a spirituality of peace : becoming human again / edited by Christian E. Early and Annmarie L. Early ; foreword by Howard Zehr.

xxiv + 152 pp. ; 23 cm. Includes bibliographical references and indexes.

ISBN 13: 978-1-62032-871-2

1. Attachment behavior. 2. Christianity—Psychology. 3. Anabaptists—Doctrines. I. Early, Christian E. II. Early, Annmarie L. III. Zehr, Howard. IV. Title.

BR110 I54 2013

Manufactured in the U.S.A.

To John Bowlby:

He dared to imagine that it was really about love.

Contents

Contributors

James Coan is Associate Professor of Psychology at the University of Virginia, Charlottesville.

Janel Curry is Provost of Gordon College, Wenham, Massachusetts.

Annmarie L. Early is Professor of Counseling at Eastern Mennonite University in Harrisonburg, Virginia.

Christian E. Early is Professor of Philosophy and Theology at Eastern Mennonite University, Harrisonburg, Virginia.

Susan Johnson is Professor of Clinical Psychology at the University of Ottowa, Canada.

Tara Kishbaugh is Associate Professor of Chemistry at Eastern Mennonite University in Harrisonburg, Virginia.

John Paul Lederach is Professor of International Peacebuilding at the University of Notre Dame, in Notre Dame, Indiana.

Nancey Murphy is Professor of Christian Philosophy at Fuller Theological Seminary in Pasadena, California.

Daniel Siegel is Clinical Professor of Psychiatry at UCLA School of Medicine in Los Angeles, California.

Howard Zehr is Distinguished Professor of Restorative Justice at Eastern Mennonite University in Harrisonburg, Virginia.

Illustrations

Foreword

BY HOWARD ZEHR

THIS BOOK IS ABOUT what it means to be human, and it may not be what you expect. Contemporary neuroscience is rapidly undermining some of our dearly held assumptions about who we are and how we function. This is not another idle academic conversation. These assumptions have been the basis of our educational and legal institutions, and changing them could have far-reaching consequences for how we structure our lives.

Western culture has primed us to think of ourselves fundamentally as individuals, with intellectual abilities that are able to function, if we try hard enough (and we really should), without undue influence from our emotions. Consequently, our educational systems are designed to teach us to learn and function alone, as competent and rational individuals. Our legal system treats us as if our actions are shaped by individual decisions for which we alone are responsible. As it is practiced today, justice is designed to be administered in an objective, rational way that treats emotions as irrelevant and suspect.

That is how we see ourselves because that is how we have been trained. As these authors demonstrate, however, we are fundamentally *relational* and *emotional*. When this reality is denied, personalities, communities, and cultures can be distorted in deeply dysfunctional ways. These distortions can in turn affect the brain, which is capable of believing the illusion of its own separateness.

In his chapter, James Coan captures it well when he declares, "Our brains are designed to be with other people." The brain expects, and is fundamentally shaped by, relationships. We are not designed to grow and develop alone, and we are not designed to solve problems by ourselves. In the words of Daniel Goleman from his important book *Social Intelligence*, we are "wired to connect."[1] This basic reality, which is increasingly confirmed by neuroscience, explains much of the personal and cultural dysfunctions we observe and experience. But it does more than just diagnose our condition: it opens up a way forward by inspiring us to envision what contexts can better provide healthy, safe spaces in which people can flourish and heal from trauma.

Attachment theory, which builds on these findings and is explored in this collection, has staggering implications for the justice arena, which is the setting of my own work. Attachment theory helps us understand the trauma often experienced by victims—trauma that motivates much of both victim and offender behavior. It explains why the dispassionate, individualized, and rationalized process of legal justice so often fails *and* why restorative justice approaches, which emphasize relationships and mutual understanding, can be so powerful.

Restorative justice processes often provide an opportunity for those who have been harmed and those who have caused harm to meet one another in a safe environment. Victim and offender have an opportunity to meet and to some extent understand each other, which can be healing. Research has found high levels of satisfaction and reduced trauma for victims who participate, and often reduced recidivism on the part of offenders. The reason this happens, I once heard a neuroscientist suggest, is that "nothing reprograms our neural pathways quicker than an experience of empathy."

Some years ago I cofacilitated a meeting between a man who had committed a series of high-profile rapes and one of the many women he had violated. Several decades had passed since their violent encounter—decades he had spent in prison. At one point in the meeting the survivor said to him, "You stole my childhood," and I saw him tear up for the first time. Later he told me that he had been through many therapeutic programs but had never understood until that moment the enormity of what he had done. He too had lost his childhood when his mother deserted the family and his father abused him. It was that experience of empathy and a moment of felt connection that got through to him.

Restorative justice—the framework of much of my own work—is based on the reality that we are interrelated. It reminds us of the web of relationships in which we are embedded and suggests principles and processes to create and restore healthy relationships. Attachment theory, with

1. Goleman, *Social Intelligence*.

its basis in psychology and neuroscience, has much to offer to my field and to many other fields as well.

This book is about making connections. The authors explore the fundamentals and implications of attachment theory. Coeditor Christian Early's commentary suggests implications for Christian theology and especially for the Anabaptist tradition that has embraced community but often has lived it poorly. As he points out, it is good and fundamentally human to live in community, but it can also be a source of great stress. That is why it is so important that "we learn to practice restoration and reconciliation, which is to say habits of repair."

Speaking to some of the global implications of attachment theory, Daniel Siegel argues that the strategy of informing and scaring people about the future of the planet hasn't worked. Instead, "we have to expand the self from 'me' to 'we' or we are dead."

How we see ourselves is an urgent moral issue. The implications of attachment theory are personal, social, and global, and that is why this book is so important.

Preface

BY TARA KISHBAUGH

WHEN THE SUGGESTION OF exploring attachment theory with an Anabaptist lens was first floated, I was immediately intrigued. As a professor of organic chemistry, I frame my classes as the study of the attraction of molecules, so the idea of attachment as a transdisciplinary paradigm that can describe the importance of forming healthy connections and reciprocal relationships seemed intuitively appealing. A cell's chance of survival hinges on how it connects to other cells, forming complex communities, tissues, and interacting systems, which are essential to its life and function. Even smaller than the cell, the molecule has physical and chemical properties determined by how it interacts with other molecules: both those that are similar to it and those that are not. What a perfect depiction of community!

Moreover, at the same time as this project was emerging, I was a new mother of a young boy. I was experiencing in a profound manner what it means to have my sense of self expanded. I was learning how to regulate the emotions of another person. I was being transformed into a secure base from which my toddler could explore his world, and to which he could return for reassurance, for love.

Finally, as a researcher, I am interested in the health of our waterways. Understanding how an ecosystem naturally functions reinforces that connections are important. Indeed, often the challenges to ecosystem health result from thinking that separates humanity from the rest of the creation or that privileges either humanity or the rest of creation. This is the heart of Lynn White's argument in "The Historical Roots of Our Ecological Crisis." He claims that Christian anthropocentrism has driven exploitation and degradation of the environment. "What people *do* about their ecology depends on what they *think* about themselves in relation to the things around them."[2] Attachment theory provides a framework for exploring environmental issues by examining our sense of self and the ways we have or have not formed healthy attachments.

I was, in short, quickly impressed both by the way that this topic transcends disciplinary boundaries and by how it provides an approachable, meaningful, and urgently important framework for understanding our world—all the way from human communities to waterways, and the molecules that hold it all together.

Shenandoah Anabaptist Science Society

In 2005 a core group of people committed to dialogue on issues at the intersection of science and religion formed the Shenandoah Anabaptist Science Society (SASS) on the campus of Eastern Mennonite University (EMU) in Harrisonburg Virginia.[3] Individuals from the community as well as from across a number of departments on campus (Biology, Chemistry, Nursing, Education, Bible and Religion, among others) joined to bring Anabaptist theological perspectives into science-and-faith discussions. A small steering committee (approximately eight members) met to organize activities designed to facilitate broad interdisciplinary dialogue, education, and action across the Harrisonburg community.

For several years we hosted speakers and facilitated book studies but did not have a central, unifying theme to our programming, but then the theme of attachment captured our collective imagination and provided an organizing concept for several years of programming. Attachment provides a biochemical, evolutionary, and psychological basis for understanding ethical virtues such as love, peace, compassion, and empathy. We noted with interest that none of the other Christian theological traditions have engaged this topic, and we came to believe that Anabaptists were uniquely suited to integrate attachment theory with our faith tradition because we have a deeply held sense of the importance of community and the importance of a reconciled relationship with God.[4]

---

2. White, "The Historical Roots of Our Ecologic Crisis." See Siegel, "Mindsight," 19 below.

3. See the web page online: www.emu.edu/sass/

4. See also Miller and Early "A Transdisciplinary Exploration of Attachment through Anabaptist Eyes" (www.emu.edu/attachment/background)."

If human beings are made in the image of God, then to view human-ity as "red in tooth and claw" is inconsistent with a loving, peaceful God who values reconciled relationships. The ethical virtues of love, empa-thy, compassion, and peace are pervasive in Anabaptist theology. Indeed when the Anabaptist community gathers, it is to discern how to follow Jesus, in a boldly humble and nonviolent manner, and to meet the needs of one another and of the wider world. This requires that we expand our sense of self and identity beyond the tribe. The Christian community then is one in which we experience *gelassenheit* or "yieldedness"—the giving of one's self to God and God's people. We discern how to reconcile broken relationships and how to form secure attachments to God and to other people. Moreover, our connections should be vibrant and secure enough to sustain a witness to peace in a violent world. The connections to at-tachment theory—with its understanding of human beings as *born to bond*—seemed, for lack of a better word, natural.

In 2009 we received funding from the Metanexus Institute, and in 2010 from the John Templeton Foundation, to begin a transdisciplinary ex-ploration of attachment theory using an Anabaptist lens. During the 2009-2010 academic year, we hosted Dr. Larry J. Young of Emory University, who described the molecular neurobiology of attachment and social bonding in voles. Dr. Nel Noddings, Professor Emeritus at Stanford University, also spoke on the ethic of care, emphasizing the importance of the dyad for excellent teaching and for improving our ethics.

In the spring of 2011 we hosted the attachment conference.[5] It was and is our hope that through the conference and now through this manuscript, we can provide clear definitions and illustrations of secure attachment and can describe the biological and psychological processes involved in emo-tional regulation. These ideas should provide the framework for:

- fostering a sense of self that expands to include others

- identifying ways to build and sustain secure connections as well as repair ruptured ones

- discovering more fully what it means for humans to thrive and to live in peace with one another and their environment

- examining an Anabaptist perspective of attachment in relationship to our churches and to God.

5. For information on the conference, see online: www.emu.edu/attachment/.

Acknowledging with Gratitude the Work of Many Hands

To thank all of the individuals and departments at EMU who participated in bringing this dream to realization would be a daunting task, but I will attempt it. Needless to say, it was a labor of love that enabled this conference to be such a success.

The impetus for this project came from Drs. Annmarie Early, Christian Early, and Roman Miller, who initially saw the potential, and whose ideas inspired this work. The group steering committee of SASS provided the early organization and centralized ideas. The membership of this group grew to reflect our intent to host a conference that transcended disciplinary boundaries. The conference-planning committee included Tara Kishbaugh, Chair (Chemistry), Katrina Alger (Development), Pam Comer (Counseling), Kenton Derstine (Seminary), Cheryl Doss (Science Center), Annmarie Early (Counseling), Christian Early (Bible & Religion), Alan Eby (a psychology instructor at Bridgewater College), John Fairfield (Anabaptist Center for Religious Studies), Ann Hershberger (Nursing), Luanne Bender Long (a local therapist), Roman Miller (Biology), Judy Mullet (Psychology), and Heidi Winters Vogel (Theater).

This group grew to include wide representation from Conferences and Auxiliary Services, the Marketing department, the Development office, the physical plant staff, the provost's office, the president's cabinet, the Information Systems department, and many others. Without the dedication, creativity, and endurance of all these people, this manuscript would not be possible.

Financial sponsorship of this ambitious project began with the Metanexus Institute and the Lilly Foundation, which provided the seed money for the formation of SASS. The Metanexus Institute also recognized the promise in the proposal, providing funding for the initial year. After the first year, the John Templeton Foundation graciously continued to administer the grant. Matching sponsorship came from Rockingham Memorial Hospital Behavioral Health, the Masters of Arts in Counseling Program, and the Student Government Association Lecture Series at Eastern Mennonite University.

For their work above and beyond expectations, we are extremely grateful to Cheryl Armstrong, Marian Bauman, Susan Beck, Craig Buller, the EMU Chamber Singers, Patty Eckard, Bruce Emmerson and the Pioneer staff, Brenda Fairweather, Stephen Gibbs, Marcy Gineris, Dave Glanzer, Phil Grayson, Jerry Holsopple, Marty King, Paul King, Stella Knicely,

Fred Kniss, Kristy Koser, B. J. Miller, Marci Myers, Ken J. Nafziger, Jenni Piper, the Print Shop, Kirk Shisler, Tony Smith, Jon Styer, Lynn Veurink, Mary Jo Veurink, Andrea Wenger, Diane Yerian, and Danny Yoder. Anca Chirvasuta and Ryan Eshleman initially transcribed the presentations and helped chase references.

Many thanks to those whose names do not appear above, yet without whose help the conference could not have been the success that it was.

Acknowledgments

ANNMARIE L. EARLY AND CHRISTIAN E. EARLY

IT ISN'T VERY OFTEN that a new idea crosses your path, impacts all aspects of your lived experience, and changes your basic understanding of how the world works. Attachment theory is that idea. At least it has played that role for us—in our marriage and in our professional work in philosophy (Christian) and psychotherapy (Annmarie); and we have come to believe that it constitutes an honest-to-goodness paradigm shift. We think it has the potential to reorient everything, and we see it as a next step for creating enriched professional conversations across disciplinary boundaries.

It was in the mid '90s that Annmarie met Dr. Susan Johnson and was trained in Emotionally Focused Therapy (EFT) for couples. As Annmarie began to shift her clinical understandings and eventually became a trainer in EFT, our conversations about attachment caught wind between us, opening up possibilities and allowing us to talk in new ways. With attachment theory, we finally had a model that no longer required complex psychodynamic explanations with structures that would often mystify Christian ("What exactly is a *permeable* self?"), and yet it accessed the very essence of lived experience in our lives. We begin our acknowledgments with gratitude to Sue Johnson for her role in introducing us to attachment, for her commitment to research and excellence, and for coming to EMU—our academic community—to share her pioneering theoretical and practical work.

It was also during this time that we were students at Fuller Theological Seminary and were introduced to Pasadena Mennonite Church (PMC) in Los Angeles. Here for the first time we learned to walk with people of the Anabaptist faith. PMC was a community with roots that were so different from our own, but we resonated with its attempt to live out its vision for peace and social justice. Under the leadership of our whimsical pastor,

Dr. Jim Brenneman, our eyes saw new potentials for relatedness. Within us Anabaptist sensibilities of creating and sustaining human community and the powerful insights afforded by attachment theory were beginning to blend and weave together. Out of the implicit blending of that season slowly came explicit conversations about spirituality and love.

We admit with candor that living within the Mennonite community in Harrisonburg is different from what we originally envisioned from our apartment in Los Angeles. This community has been a rich learning landscape that has been both our home and teacher. Part of what made this conference so compelling is that it was housed here at EMU. On this campus people gather together with a commitment to give voice in conversation. We treasure the voice of the whole—from those who work in the administrative suite to those who keep our campus beautiful. (It is, after all, in the Shenandoah Valley.) Communal discernment and decision making can sometimes be long in coming—pacifism, to state the obvious, requires patience—because it values all voices in charting a pathway forward. But, this implicit value creates an atmosphere alive with possibility and many who visit EMU feel it in the very landscape speaking clearly of the uniqueness of this community. As an African proverb has it, "Slowly, slowly, the egg will walk."

There would never have been a campus-wide conversation about attachment theory and Anabaptism without the visioning leadership and the practical direction of Dr. Roman Miller, who wrote the grant to Metanexus with Christian, without the tireless and capable leadership of Dr. Tara Kishbaugh, who has steered Shenandoah Anabaptist Science Society through rough weather, and without the unfailing support of EMU leadership, including President Dr. Loren Swartzendruber and Provost Dr. Fred Kniss—especially when funding threatened to disappear. Once the grant was in hand, and Christian had a firm hold on the conference theme, we had such fun imagining who we would want to bring together from our intellectual community for this conference. We dreamed of the best in their respective fields and are so grateful that they all said yes. Thank you to Sue Johnson, Dan Siegel, Jim Coan, John Paul Lederach, and Nancey Murphy for coming and sharing with us. As we have reread and edited this volume, we are more convinced now than ever that what these leaders have to say is current, relevant, and inspirational for creating change in the larger world.

It was an enormous task to host a conference of this size. We are especially grateful to Tara Kishbaugh and to Cheryl Doss, who both carried the burden of holding all the details. They created the infrastructure that made the event possible. There was support across campus from faculty to physical plant staff—who all worked to make the event happen. We want to say thank you to each one of you, and we feel personally grateful to you.

Finally, we wish to express our gratitude to John Bowlby, to whom we dedicate this volume. He faced great scorn and ridicule from his professional community as he spoke of the importance of actual human relationship in our overall well-being. It is our hope that following Bowlby's example, we might find new and more ways to give voice to the reality of love and the vision of peace—in the face of criticism, which belongs, it all belongs—acknowledging the higher calling of genuine connection that has the power to overcome and transform. What better conversation to engage than the one between a faith tradition that has sought to embody the way of Jesus of Nazareth and a scientific theory that helps us to understand why it makes a difference. With *Integrating the New Science of Love and a Spirituality of Peace*, we invite readers to find your own next steps from which to engage this conversation.

1

Introduction

ANNMARIE L. EARLY AND CHRISTIAN E. EARLY

FOR A WHILE NOW, religion and science have been uncomfortable bed-fellows, but it was not always so, and there is good reason to think that it may not continue to be so in the near future either: our cosmological and anthropological paradigms are shifting, allowing for new conversations between disciplines, and new stories of what it means to be human.[1] A brief recap and some stage setting may be in order.

Science and Religion in Tension

The tension began at least as far back as when the medieval synthesis between Christian theology and Platonic and Aristotelian philosophy ceased to be persuasive, which is to say at the beginning of the modern scientific revolution.[2] In his *Dialogues Concerning Two Chief World Systems: Ptolemaic and Copernican* (1632), Galileo Galilei effectively undermined the claim that we needed such things as essences or forms in order to make sense of the world, and fifty-some years later Isaac Newton showed in his *Philosophiae Naturalis Principia Mathematica* (1687) that the motion of

---

1. For shifts in cosmology, see for example Kauffman, *Reinventing the Sacred*; and Prigogine, *The End of Certainty*.

2. It is an oversimplification to say that the tensions began with the dissolution of the medieval synthesis, because there has always been a tension between believing in things and wondering whether they are really so, but this is one place where we can pick up the story.

terrestrial and celestial bodies could be explained using concepts of force and matter and understanding their mathematical relation.[3]

The old theological doctrine of the two books (the book of Scripture and the book of creation, both thought to be written by God) became largely unusable because science could no longer serve as a foreword to theology. Slowly but surely science seemed to suggest that even if there were a God, God did not participate actively in the events of the universe. Perhaps it would be simpler to do away with God as a hypothesis anyway since it (the hypothesis, that is) seemed to raise far more problems than it solved (chief among which was the way God was enlisted into the various warring factions of post-Christendom Europe).

Modern materialism, however, was not without its own problems. If force and matter were the only concepts needed to explain events, then what would become of the human being? Either the human being is folded into the universe and is governed by natural law like everything else, or the human being is pushed to the margins of the universe, and the anomaly of free will is momentarily tolerated. Moreover, as Albert Camus saw clearer than perhaps anyone else, if the universe did not care about the human condition, and if the idea of God's plan unfolding in human history was becoming a cruel joke, then the inescapable existential question centered on the crisis of meaning. If caring is purely artificial—the quixotic drive of medicine, let's say, which, when it cannot cure a disease, doesn't quite know what to do with the human person except kill the pain—but not *natural* in some sense, then we start to ask questions about the point of it all.

3. See Galileo, *Dialogue Concerning Two Chief World Systems*; and Newton, *The Principia*. While we are on the subject, we might parenthetically note a nagging problem at the core of Newton's ideas: if matter was inert, as he claimed, then whence does the force of gravity come, and how on earth (we might be permitted to ask) does it act at a distance? Gravitational pull seems very much like something matter does without touching anything, and since Newton's theory of action and his definition of matter necessitate that forms of matter come into contact, the effects of gravity become somewhat spooky. One way to understand Einstein is to see that he provides an account of movement that does not appeal to action at a distance but rather to the curvature of space-time—bodies move along geodesics. Einstein is an improvement over Newton, but the thought of the curvature of space-time strikes most of us a somewhat counterintuitive and tends to stretch our minds just a bit beyond our reach.

Darwin's Discovery of Emotion

There had been scientific advances too on the anthropological front. In his justly famous *On the Origin of Species* (1859), Charles Darwin argued that the nearly infinite diversity of species we see around us could be very neatly explained with the concept of evolution by means of natural selection.[4] Darwin had no need for the guiding hand of God here either. Darwin's ideas, perhaps more than any other scientist's, have sparked numerous debates. (The debates happen not just in academic circles either, so some have been tempted to call the standoff a cultural war.) Darwin's ideas cause controversy in part because evolutionary theory has been overwhelmingly confirmed by the discovery of genes, and natural selection seems to be able to explain much more than just biodiversity.

Darwin himself, to his credit, did not stop tinkering with his own understanding of what it meant to be human and to be alive. Through ethology (including of the human animal), he noticed that we have (and share) a rich emotional life.[5] He noticed, for example, cows contentedly frisking about and throwing around their tails from pleasure. It is hard to imagine Darwin not chuckling just a little to himself at the sight of an obviously happy cow. By paying close attention to the body and its movements, Darwin discovered the *inner world* of animals, and this may have been his most important discovery because it changed his sense of what it meant to be alive. (One could wish that it would change Richard Dawkins's sense too: here as in other places, the problem isn't being a Darwinian; the problem is not being Darwinian enough.)[6] Instead of thinking about our lived situation as always and only selfishly competitive, Darwin began to see that it was much better characterized as a stage for social connection and emotions: playfulness, caring, anger, sadness, fear, and laughter.

4. Darwin, *On the Origin of Species*.

5. Darwin, *The Expression of the Emotions in Man and Animals*.

6. Dawkins, *The Selfish Gene*. One way to get at the shift in Darwin, perhaps, is to say that animal life suddenly gained the dimension of depth. Gaining the dimension of depth is not merely something added to the picture. It changes everything. In his *Against Method*, Paul Feyerabend discusses the incommensurability between Greek Archaic art (characterized by paratactic aggregates) and Greek Classical art (characterized by hypotactic connections). The eye is suddenly *looking*, which signals not just a change in artistic skill but a change in cosmology (see *Against Method*, chapter 16). We might say that as a result of ethology, Darwin went through a similar transition.

Bowlby and Attachment Theory

Regrettably, very few picked up Darwin's work on emotion.[7] Europe and the world threw itself first into one devastating war and then another. Emotions seemed like dangerous things—best kept at bay, preferably eliminated, and certainly not studied—until John Bowlby happened to notice them.[8] Working with children and their caregivers, and studying of children orphaned in the aftermath of the World War II, John Bowlby argued that lack of sufficient human connection during early development had predictable life-altering ramifications. His work showed that insufficient caregiving and, specifically, maternal deprivation, in the early stages of life has deleterious effects and in the most extreme cases leads to psychopathology and deviant behavior. More generally, Bowlby's research demonstrated that lack of secure connection with a caregiver creates distress and leads to styles of relating that impact overall human social functioning and thriving. And, as stated above, in extreme situations where detachment occurs, a form of disconnection colored by a lack of empathy can develop, allowing an individual to perpetrate violence without remorse.[9]

Scorned by his peers, who in the grips of Freudianism valued drives and the symbolic, internalized world above lived experience, Bowlby was challenged to articulate a theory of attachment that documented the consequences of the lived experience of children and their caregivers.[10] Research by Mary Ainsworth (the Strange Situation) and by Mary Main (the Adult Attachment Interview) brought some credibility to attachment theory, but its acceptance outside the field of child development has been delayed until recently.[11] Contemporary neuroscience and fMRI studies now allow us to see the brain in action, and what we are seeing confirms Bowlby's theory of attachment. Like evolutionary theory, attachment theory has become a metaframework and has created a paradigmatic shift in how we see ourselves and how we understand our need for connection with other beings.

Attachment is most basically about the ability to regulate emotion during times of distress. Extending Darwin's later insights, Bowlby realized

7. William James and Sigmund Freud are notable exceptions.

8. It is interesting that Bowlby wrote a biography of Darwin; see Bowlby, *Charles Darwin.*

9. See Bowlby, *A Secure Base*; and Schore, "The Effects of Early Relational Trauma."

10. See Bowlby, *Attachment and Loss,* vols. 1–3.

11. See Ainsworth et al., "Patterns of Attachment"; and Main et al., "Studying Difference in Language Usage in Recounting Attachment History."

that while the constant struggle to stay alive persists, the fundamental way that humans (and other animals) deal with that stress is through social connection, not competition. Moreover, the social implications of lack of attachment are multitudinous. Attachment is about the capacity to *be there when needed*. Attachment theory recognizes that contact (proximity seeking) during times of stress is crucial. Key moments of need *define* relationships as either safe or dangerous, and consequently shift relational dynamics. Bonding happens when a person reaches out for contact during a perceived stress and makes contact with the intended other. These bonds are powerful and persuasive, often overriding previous relational cues. Successful connection during a moment of need creates bonding. A moment of disconnection during a time of stress, however, signals danger and the need to protect. The communication is limbic and split-second fast; the motivation and emotion system sends a very quick alert response in the midbrain, which motivates the organism for action.[12] These bottom-up signals are powerful, shifting dynamics in the moment and potentially influencing behavior over the lifespan.

Current research overwhelmingly supports Bowlby's articulation of attachment theory as a proximity-seeking system especially active during times of distress when we need help regulating our emotions, and we are just now beginning to grasp the full implications and applications.[13] For starters, the confirmation of attachment theory puts us in a position to say that we are fundamentally relational and emotional beings, not rational and calculating individuals as modern Enlightenment theorists thought.[14] Now we can begin to understand with theoretical specificity the devastating consequences of disconnection: its influence not only in the makeup of a human being, but also on the large scale of the social tragedies and traumas that plague our world today.

But there is much more here. As a lens through which to understand human behavior and psychology, attachment theory offers a runway from which to launch new research projects and to explore the dynamics of interaction and encounter. Imagining into new ways of engaging the within

12. See Schore, "Right Brain Affect Regulation."

13. See Cassidy and Shaver, *Handbook of Attachment*; and Mikulincer and Shaver, *Attachment in Adulthood*.

14. This should not be understood as if humans are irrational. Rather, reason and emotion need to be understood as not being mutually exclusive opposites. An emotion, for example, includes an appraisal of a situation, and in anatomical terms the brain systems required by emotion and reason are enmeshed. See Damasio, *Descartes' Error*.

and between of connection by addressing social policy, where the way we live is addressed. Finally, it is our faith communities that (when they are at their best) demonstrate the story of connection in sacred text and in the lived story of the community as safe haven and secure base.

A New Conversation between Science and Religion

In that context, Anabaptism offers a distinct perspective, with its vision for what it means to be human together, with its emphasis on concrete embodied community, on being there when needed, on yielding to God's call and trusting in God's presence in times of stress, and with its commitment to pacifism.[15] Anabaptism has not historically been in the limelight, not other than as the object of persecution and confessional rebuke, but it may be a more fruitful conversation partner with the science of attachment theory than other theological traditions.[16]

The vision of the kingdom of God as taught by Jesus of Nazareth, which Anabaptism holds at its center, is very clearly enriched by understanding the importance of communal connection, the key aspects that create safety, and the consequences of disconnection especially during times of need or stress. Many of the communal practices such as foot washing, barn raising, providing meals for those in need, and intervening internationally in contexts of trauma and tragedy create essential elements for secure attachment. It is the actual embodied presence, the *being there when needed*, that takes a potentially threatening and dangerous situation and creates lasting connections, which change the neurochemistry of the body and transform social conflict.

Attachment theory also has something to gain from Anabaptism. Specifically, attachment theory can expand its analysis from the dynamics of mother–infant and partner–partner relationships into the territory of community building and social-conflict studies. As it does so, it is unlikely that it will stay entirely the same. A new kind of religion-and-science conversation is now possible, as scientific disciplines reconsider what it means to be human, and as faith communities try to understand what it means to

15. See Yoder, *Body Politics*.

16. Because it does not take its cue from Augustine, Anabaptism does not begin its theological anthropology with a doctrine of original sin. This does not mean that Anabaptists are not well attuned to the ways in which human interactions can go horribly wrong. (They were, after all, burned at the stake for heresy.) It means rather that human interactions do not *need* to go horribly wrong.

be followers of Jesus of Nazareth. Perhaps the conversation shouldn't strike us as quite so surprising since a favorite way for the authors of the Gospels to name Jesus was as the Son of the Human, or less literally but more accurately, as the *Truly Human One*.[17]

The time is ripe for change, and an encounter between the Anabaptism and attachment theory might be the kind of conversation with precisely that potential. It requires, however, that we engage our own story with openness and self-reflective honesty. (Such engagement is required especially from those with Anabaptist convictions and with ethnic Mennonite heritage; these authors do not share that heritage). We are required to talk about the shadow side of community. The Anabaptist story contains deep experiences of trauma and tragedy—not just the historically documented ones from without, which are publicly remembered, but the undocumented ones from within as well, which are hidden. Attachment theory offers a fresh way to engage the painful sides of the story and suggests ways of moving towards healing and restoration. Moreover, Mennonites more than most enjoy the felt safety of connection established over generations, but it is a connection that, while it generously invites the outsider in, erects invisible walls felt by those not born into the community. Reflecting anew on the rich story of Anabaptism—on its triumphs and tragedies—can offer solid ground from which to pursue nonviolent engagement and encounter with the larger world, even the one in our own communities.

Conversations on Attachment

The conference Conversations on Attachment: Integrating the Science of Love and Spirituality, hosted by Eastern Mennonite University (EMU) and the Shenandoah Anabaptist Science Society, offered our Anabaptist community the opportunity to engage current attachment-theory findings,

17. Note that the previous conversation between science and religion often centered on accounts of cause and effect and terms such as *design* and *law* to determine whether God was needed to explain the data. Thus was born the "God of the gaps," a god who was invented (first, ironically, by theologians) to explain whatever was left over that mechanistic explanations could not (yet) explain, and who was forever on the retreat, giving the false impression that as the explanatory power of scientific theories increases, so the need for religious explanations decreases and eventually will disappear. Now, however, we are having a conversation, largely driven by advances in neuroscience, concerning what it means to be human. Here, it turns out, religious traditions have a lot to contribute, and that contribution is constructive and collaborative (not competitive) *with* science.

advances in neuroscience, ethics, as well as stories of love within dyadic and communal relationships, in order to understand better what *we* do and to help think of ourselves as a safe haven for the world and as a secure base from which to offer service in the ways of Jesus.

In the following pages, the conference keynotes are presented, followed by short reflective responses from Christian, just as they were presented during the event. An additional article on attachment and place is included to contextualize possible applications of attachment not only in relationships but also in context and space. The keynotes have been reordered to allow readers to follow the thematic development from science to application, hopefully encouraging personal reflection on next steps in furthering the discussion.

Setting the stage is Daniel Siegel, Professor of Clinical Psychiatry at the UCLA School of Medicine, where he is on faculty at the Center for Culture, Brain, and Development. Siegel has authored many popular books, including *The Developing Mind* and *Mindsight*. Siegel lays out the neuroscience of attachment and emphasizes the specific importance of understanding brain processes and how they impact our engagement with others and the world.[18] He argues that the self emerges out of our interaction with other people (the *feeling felt* of lived experience). Siegel describes the importance of the limbic brain in the following processes: emotion regulation; memory generation; fight, flight, and freeze responses; and (especially) attachment. Siegel treats the role of emotion regulation in emotional balance: internal states create a context where life is vital and rich. Moreover, he discusses the imperative of practicing mindsight (regularly activating the resonance circuit that allows connection with other humans), which has implications for morality and ethics.

Gathering the pieces together, he calls his research program Interpersonal Neurobiology. It emphasizes the importance of attachment relationships that promote integration, which is the linking of differentiated parts, because an integrated mind is a healthy mind. Siegel imagines a river of integration within which the sharing of energy and information flows between chaos (no linking between differentiated parts) and rigidity (no differentiated parts between the links). Here we become aware of a spiritual place he calls the "plane of possibility": "where hope arises, where compassion is born, and where our deep sense of attachment and connection to each other arises, so that we can bring more love and compassion into this world."[19]

18. Siegel, *The Developing Mind*; and Siegel, *Mindsight*.
19. See Siegel, "From Me to We," 30–43 below.

James Coan, a neuroscientist at the University of Virginia and author of the hand-holding study, argues that humans are like other mammals in their capacity to regulate through social contact and proximity, a resource-conserving strategy, but unlike other animals we also have the ability to regulate our emotions through the use of our prefrontal cortex: a very effective but very costly strategy. The research from his hand-holding studies shows that during times of stress we function better when others are present than when we face life alone. (Others help us self-regulate, and we don't have to solve as many problems.) This is the "social regulation of emotion," and it is the way most mammals navigate the upheavals of life, but Coan goes beyond that to propose what he calls *social-baseline theory.*

Instead of viewing social connection as depressing problems to be solved (presupposing that the individual is the baseline), social-baseline theory claims that social disconnection creates more problems to be solved (presupposing that the socially connected being is the baseline). Moreover, social-baseline theory is corroborated by perception studies in the economy of action. Coan goes on to expand our understanding of the self beyond the walls of the body to include others and our community as part of what we call the self. Social-baseline theory consequently has implications for how we understand our sense of self, our relationships, our community, our connections, and ultimately our view of spirituality.

Susan Johnson, author of *Hold Me Tight* and leading couples-therapy researcher and originator of Emotionally Focused Couples Therapy, an evidence-based, empirically validated approach to treating couples distress, shares research that supports a new science of love and adult bonding demonstrating how connection impacts the way in which we see ourselves in the world.[20] Her extensive research integrates a focus on both the self and dyadic dynamics, highlighting emotional connection and the circular interaction patterns that establish either safe connection or insecurity in love relationships.

Johnson argues that if you are able to reach out to a loved one and they respond, you can establish safe haven security. She uses the attachment literature to show that this is our most primary need and mediates the effects of emotional isolation, allowing individuals to be more fully functioning and have greater satisfaction and stability in their relationships. The research shows that happy marriages are built on the rhythm of rupture and repair in which secure couples can reach for each other during times

20. See Johnson, *Hold Me Tight*; and Johnson, *Creating Connection.*

of need. Relational repair alleviates attachment panic and floods us with powerful positive emotions such as joy and contentment. Our adult love relationships are similar to the mother repairing with her infant, built on the reciprocal emotional openness of a safe emotional bond. Johnson shows that our new science takes the mystery out of what makes relationships successful and helps partners establish meaningful, long-lasting connection.

John Paul Lederach, Professor of International Peacebuilding at the University of Notre Dame and internationally recognized leader in the field of conflict transformation, leads us through the story of Balu—an ex-bonded slave—and his journey to gain voice in a situation of deep conflict. Lederach outlines the power of listening (*dadirri*) and the way in which "people story themselves back into place." He describes how conflict-transformation workers listen by focusing on the deeper story that moves beyond voicelessness and too much noise. He opens a place of possibility where a vibration of sound penetrates through: "it touches you inside, and you feel it in your bones."[21] Lederach captures the quality of this vibration where attachment theory and conflict transformation meet through the lived stories of listening and in the metaphor of the singing bowl, moving voicelessness into penetrating proxemics, where a portal for connection is birthed, and the harmonics of connection bubble with possibility. Lederach uses story as a way to speak, to give voice, allowing readers to inhabit the narrative in an embodied way.

Nancey Murphy, internationally recognized speaker and author of the award-winning *Theology in the Age of Scientific Reasoning* as well as many other books in the area of philosophy and theology, most recently *Did My Neurons Make Me Do It?*, argues that the emergent understanding of the self in the attachment literature marks, finally, a departure from the understanding of the self that we have inherited from Augustine and later Hobbes.[22] She notes that this new understanding happens to fit very nicely with the understanding of the human person in the Old and New Testaments, and it even helps us to make sense of certain passages that before were mysterious. She ends with a discussion concerning the fit between attachment theory and Anabaptism. She describes some of the many practices of the Anabaptists such as believer's baptism, community discipline, communion, foot washing, discernment, and the overcoming of walls of human separation in the promise of a new creation. This shared way of life—and with the lens of attachment theory, we can now understand why the practices were so powerful—raises

21. See Lederach, "Narratives of Care, 84 below.

22. Murphy, *Theology in the Age of Scientific Reasoning*; and Murphy, *Did My Neurons Make Me Do It?*

a crucial theological question with respect to our understanding of God and ultimate reality. The short answer is that God is Love, a love that flows out not just to neighbors but to enemies too. Jesus invites us to embed ourselves, as he did, into our heavenly Father, and we will never be alone.

Janel Curry is Provost of Gordon College but a geographer by training. Her research focuses on the intersection of society and nature, and some of her favorite landscapes include the Palouse Hills of Washington and the Swan River Valley of Manitoba. She points out that while the link between early secure attachment and later adult capacity to form secure relationships is becoming well understood, the same link may apply to relationships between humans and nature, but this has not yet been appreciated much less studied. Part of the problem has been that our understanding of nature is not yet rich enough to capture the multifaceted aspects of this relationship. She points to the vision of these relationships found in Aldo Leopold's land ethic, where he asks us to enlarge the boundaries of our concept of community to include the natural world. In seeing ourselves and acting as a member of this larger community, which now includes the environment, we can begin to talk about the dynamics of dependency and interdependency, that is of the dynamics of our attachment with other individuals, the human community, and the natural world.

We End with Song

During the conference, numerous breakout sessions were weaved throughout the three-day conference offering opportunities for discipline-specific engagement and conversation as well as opportunities to join together in corporate voice in an embodied experience of integration, led by Ken J. Nafziger. Together we felt our way into an emergent song, requiring attunement and resonance that built on harmonies of over a thousand voices. As we sang our way into creation, we felt bodily the power of integration. It is our hope that this book will provide a space for resonant conversation, not arriving at a conclusion or position, but rather opening the space for new voices to share and consider, opening a space that speaks forth honoring the spirit of the "plane of possibility,"[23] where we are able to attune to one another with openness and receptivity, hearing deeply the story of connection told for generations in sacred texts and the everyday story of our lives.

23. See Siegel, *Mindsight.*

2

Mindsight

Transforming a Sense of Self in the World

DANIEL SIEGEL

I N THIS CHAPTER, I will discuss recent understandings of relationships, the mind, and the brain, looking at attachment in a little more depth. Then I would like to raise some fundamental questions about the idea of spirituality. It was not too long ago that I had never addressed spirituality, whether at a conference or in writing. In the last few years, however, I have gotten more requests to speak at spirituality conferences than at almost any other kind of conference. We are participating in an amazing moment in history, in which the spiritual quest in religious communities is again making contact with the fields of science: the gap between spirituality and science has for so long been an impassable divide.

Leanne and Barbara's Story

I want to begin with a story about a family that changed my life. As a child psychiatrist, I (of course) see children. Years ago, before any of the things I will share today were written, I was taking care of a seven-year-old girl whom we will call Leanne. Leanne had stopped speaking in school, refusing to talk to anyone. Her father and mother brought her in for an evaluation, and of course she did not say anything to me either.

I started an extensive evaluation of Leanne by playing with her in silence. During the evaluation, a ball with which we were playing catch went behind the couch where there was a video player. Leanne became very animated. I asked her whether she would like to bring something into our next session, and she nodded her head slightly. The next week she came in bringing a cassette. We put the cassette in the video machine, and there on the screen was a video that her father had made from two years before. In the video you see this exquisite five-year old girl and her mother in a relational dance. It was very much like the Ed Tronick video of the baby and mother who beautifully demonstrate this dance of attunement before the still-face experiment.[1] This kind of attunement is an incredible connection, where the sense of self emerges from our interaction with other people—*self* becomes more like a plural verb than a singular noun. You could see this with Leanne and her mom. They were attuned and connected. You could see that the mom could feel her daughter inside her own body, and that in that moment Leanne herself was experiencing a feeling of being felt. Leanne knew that everything was safe and the world was at ease.

Leanne's mother, who was sitting in my waiting room (we will call her Barbara), was not the same woman. Barbara had had a terrible car accident about a year before Leanne first came to see me for an evaluation. During Barbara's short trip to the store to get milk, a drunk teenage driver hit her head-on. Unfortunately, Barbara had not put on a safety belt, and the car she was driving did not have air bags. The steering wheel of the car plowed into Barbara's skull and severely damaged a part of her brain just behind the forehead. Barbara had brain surgery to remove the shards of bone and plastic surgery to allow her to look much like what she had before. After being in a coma and residency at a rehabilitation center, Barbara returned home, and that is when Leanne stopped speaking.

We can wonder why a daughter, now six and a half, would stop speaking when her mom came back from such an ordeal. What was going on? A clue was that the woman in the waiting room was so different from the woman in the tape. Barbara seemed apathetic. She would have abrupt eruptions of emotion and would get easily irritable with Leanne. Soon, I would see the entire family, including the husband and the two other siblings, and by their reports she was today nothing like the woman that I heard about or saw in the videotape.

Searching for an explanation, I asked Barbara's neurosurgeon to send me the scans of her brain. Then, I marched over to the UCLA medical school library and I researched. I picked out books and sat down with the scans, poring over all the research studies that discussed the areas of the

1. See Tronick, *The Still Face Experiment.*

brain damaged in her accident.[2] Back in the early '90s, we had a general sense what those areas of the brain allowed us to do, and I started to compile a list, which ultimately became a bit longer, that included nine functions of the damaged areas. Here is the list:[3]

1. Body regulation

2. Attuned communication

3. Emotion regulation

4. Response flexibility

5. Fear modulation

6. Insight

7. Empathy

8. Morality

9. Intuition

If the prefrontal cortex is damaged, as it was in Barbara's accident, these functions are severely impaired. (Sometimes they are impaired even if you are just a sleep-deprived parent.)

A Brief Look at the Brain

It may be helpful to say a little bit about three important areas of the brain. The first area of the brain is the brainstem. The brainstem is the deepest, oldest part of the brain. It is sometimes called the reptilian part of the brain. It first develops in utero and helps regulate bodily states such as the heart and lungs. It also has clusters of neurons called nuclei that control the fight/flight/freeze response, and it works with the rest of the brain to mediate those responses.

2. The simplest thing would be for us to call it the prefrontal cortex. There are lots of areas in the cortex, and the whole brain part of the nervous system has about a hundred billion neurons. If we were going to be perfectly respectful, we would name every one of those neurons, but they work together as clusters. They group together in nuclei, circuits, hemispheres, the whole cortex, and in fact these hundred billion neurons are interconnected with the entire body. Just as it makes no sense to talk about a self separate from a social context, it really never makes sense to talk about a brain separate from a body. I will use the word *brain*, but I mean the embodied brain, and we can say *prefrontal cortex*, but we mean a cluster of interconnected neurons.

3. For a more detailed discussion of brain functioning, see www.dr.dansiegel.com/.

Next is the limbic area. This area evolved about two hundred million years ago when we became mammals. The limbic area has the amygdala and the hippocampus. It works closely with the brainstem and body to generate emotion.[4] It helps regulate motivational systems.[5] It works with the brainstem in reproduction, affiliation, and resource allocation. It also appraises situations, assessing whether what is happening right now is worth paying attention to. Should I orient my attention to it? We call that primary appraisal. Secondary appraisal assesses whether what is happening is good or bad. If it is good, then I want to get more of it, and I want to go toward it. If it is bad, then I want to get away from it. If it is really bad (a threat, for instance), then I will generate a fight, flight, or freeze response.

The brain's concern with safety and danger deserves a special comment. It turns out that there is intricate communication between the brainstem, the limbic area, and the prefrontal area that constantly is involved in the evaluation for danger. This vigilance is exhausting if you never feel any relief. How do you achieve a sense of relief from the vigilance for danger? Part of the answer at least is through social engagement and attachment.[6]

The limbic area also generates different kinds of memory: emotional memories, bodily memories, and something called explicit memory, for which the hippocampus is very important. Finally, the limbic area is essential for attachment. I have raised fish, frogs, lizards, dogs, and children. I can tell you from personal experience that mammals have attachment and fish do not. The reason is that attachment is limbically mediated, and mammals have a limbic region whereas fish do not.

The third, and outer part of the brain, is called the cortex. The cortex also developed from our mammalian heritage, and like the limbic area it is about two hundred million years old. The more frontal areas of the cortex evolved when we became primates, and the front-front area is called the prefrontal area. The cortex maps things, and in brain terms a map is a neural firing pattern that stands for something. So, for example, the occipital cortex

4. To the best of my knowledge, there is no agreement yet among scientists working in this area about how to define emotion or even what an emotion is. This does not imply that emotions are not real; it simply means that we have more work to do in terms of our understanding of emotions. In general, while we ought to be scientifically consistent, we need not be constrained by the current lack of consensus or research. See Siegel, *The Developing Mind*.

5. See Panksepp, *Affective Neuroscience*.

6. See Porges, *Polyvagal Theory*.

maps three-dimensional space however you can get it.[7] Your motor cortex determines how you voluntarily move your limbs. Once you get to premotor planning, however, you are making a map of the future, and then the whole game changes because at that point you are creating imagination. In general, it is a useful overgeneralization to say that the back of the brain generally maps out the physical world of external reality and our body in space, but the further towards the front you go, the more conceptual the mapping is, and the more distance you get from being anchored in the three-dimensional reality. As an example, the prefrontal cortex area allows you to connect the past, the present, and the future, thereby creating a sense of self.

On Genes, Experience, Brain, and Culture

I help run the Center for Culture, Brain, and Development at UCLA.[8] We have been in existence for about ten years now, and we do research that looks at the way social practices shape the synaptic connections in the developing brain. It is also true, of course, that our genes shape the brain.[9] Genes are very important for how neurons get connected. However, once a baby is born, and even before, experience also plays a role—not instead of genes, but in addition to genes—so that we are never pitting genes against experience. Something like temperament is thought to exist in large part due to your genetic inheritance, but attachment relationships, which are part of your lived experience, have a profound effect on how the not yet wired parts of the brain will get wired up.

There is a simple reason why this is so. Whereas the brainstem is highly developed in utero, the limbic area is only partially developed, which means that the connections too are only partially there. The narrowness of human hips allow us to walk upright, but because of the largeness of the human head, the baby essentially comes out too early. I used to raise guinea pigs. Those pigs would come out, and they would be ready to eat within a few hours. Now they were chewing blind for a while, but they were out there. We as humans are very dependent—not just interdependent—on our

---

7. We used to call it the visual cortex, but we do not do that anymore because we know if we put you in a house and blindfolded you for a week or two, your fingers would have taken over that area of the brain.

8. Online: www.cbd.ucla.edu/.

9. See LeDoux, *The Synaptic Self.*

parents for considerably longer.[10] The human cortex is extremely under-developed at birth, which means that experience will shape how the brain develops. We talk about neuroplasticity, which is a name for the way experience continues to shape the architecture and connections of the brain.

Back to Barbara

Now let's look at what happened when Barbara had her accident. Something profound happened to her prefrontal cortex such that Leanne and the other children became emotionally distraught. Barbara was alive, and she looked physically the same, but she had lost crucial brain functions. These lost brain functions tell us something important about the human condition.

First, Barbara lost the ability to regulate her body, especially her heart and her intestines, which in turn impacted her ability to create and sustain attuned communication. Attuned communication is the basic way in which one human being focuses in on the internal experience of another person as expressed by their (often) nonverbal signals: eye contact, facial expression, tone of voice, posture, gestures, timing, and intensity of response. If we all remembered how to communicate nonverbally (because having language, we tend to forget it), we would have a different world. As Tronick shows, babies thrive on nonverbal communication.[11] A still face blocks nonverbal communication, which you can think of as the energy flow from internal states of one person to another. Communication is the basis of a relationship, so if you block the sharing of energy and information flow, then you have blocked the relationship.

Attuned communication requires this prefrontal area. Since Barbara lost this brain function, her children were living in a perpetual still-face experiment. Thankfully, because they were older they had the benefit of years of attunement. In Leanne's case, she had six years of being with an unbelievably attuned mother. This allowed Leanne to develop at least some autonomous self-regulation: *self-regulation*, as the word suggests, is the ability to regulate yourself, but the word *autonomous* is a bit of a misnomer because we are never totally independent of each other. We always need each other.

What else did Barbara lose? She lost emotion regulation. Emotion regulation can also be called emotional balance. This means that our internal

10. About thirty-five years or so?

11. See Tronick, *The Neurobehavioral and Socio-Emotional Development of Infants and Children.*

states are revved up enough so that life has vitality, but not revved up so much that it becomes chaotic, or so depleted that it becomes depressed. This optimal flow between chaos on the one hand and rigidity on the other is emotional balance, or emotional regulation. Another aspect is response flexibility, which is your capacity to pause before acting on an impulse. Response flexibility allows one to take a sacred pause, opening the space of mind to more options for responsive action. Wouldn't it be amazing if the planet had people who had response flexibility?

Barbara lost fear modulation. There are axonal connections from the prefrontal area down to the amygdala that secrete inhibitory peptides. If those connections are damaged then you get fear, which you have overcome, returning. That is fear modulation.

Barbara lost her capacity for insight. *Insight* is the word I use for what Endel Tulving calls mental time travel.[12] It is the ability to reflect on the past, know how it influences you in the present, and imagine the kind of future you would like to have. Insight, or mental time travel, is an important way in which you map out a temporal sense of me, or a map of me for short. I call the insight that we gain from constructing a map of me "mindsight."[13]

Barbara lost her capacity for empathy. A different part of the prefrontal area makes a mindsight map of you. Empathy gets what is going on for you in your subjective reality. Although there are at least nine different ways of defining *empathy*, we will use this one to describe what Barbara had lost.

Barbara lost morality and an underlying sense of self that is greater than her skin. The prefrontal cortex makes a map of me and a map of you, but I want to suggest to you that it also makes a mindsight map of *we*. A mindsight map of *we* thinks about the common good to a sense of self that not only reaches out to others but also defines itself as a part of *we*. It is the sense that I am more than me: I am connected to you and I am we.

Finally, Barbara lost her capacity for intuition. She no longer had access to her bodily input. Believe it or not, the intestines and the heart have massive neural net processors around them that process information and give you the wisdom of the body. It is more than a poetic metaphor. Literally, these signals go up an area of the spinal cord, and they inform especially the right hemisphere of the nonrational but incredibly important intuitive way of knowing.[14]

12. See Tulving, *Elements of Episodic Memory.*
13. See Siegel, *Mindsight.*
14. See McGilchrist, *The Master and His Emissary.*

Expanding Our Sense of Self

Let me say a bit more about a sense of self that is greater than your own skin, and its connection to health and morality because I believe this is so important. Currently, I am part of a project in which we are teaching school kids from pre-K on to have a sense of self that is not limited to the body. We believe that the culture of a school can have a huge impact on the well-being of children—especially when the parents are involved. Every study of happiness, wisdom, and health that I know of suggests that well-being comes along with a sense of the self connected to a much larger entity than the body.

It is a curious thing. Why should this body feel that it has a monopoly on this thing called Dan? There is absolutely no reason, except that our culture for perhaps the last fifteen hundred years has evoked a sense of self as separate. At the Center for Culture, Brain, and Development, we are showing that these messages from culture impact the way the brain functions. To put it simply, the human brain is very susceptible to the communication that it receives from other people within cultures. So if you have centuries of a cultural message the self is separate, then of course it has an impact.

Einstein famously talked about the *optical delusion* of our separateness. We know that the brain is capable of having the view, to which it holds on for dear life, that the self is limited to the skin. That is the cultural message. The self that is limited to the skin has this deep feeling that something is missing. So you want to buy and consume, get more and bigger stuff. The consequence, however, is that we are killing the planet with our consumption.

I work with the Garrison Institute Climate, Mind, and Behavior Project in New York. Without giving you the details, our situation as a species on planet earth is dire. I am no expert in climate-change issues, so I wondered what I could contribute to the conversation. The organizers explained to me that they were exploring other options to share their message, because apparently neither scaring people nor informing people works. The only message I could offer was this: if we don't change the cultural message that the self is more than the skin, then we are doomed. You have to expand the notion of a sense of self from *me* to *we*, or we are dead. That inspired them! (Not the dead part, because they live with that.) If you see that we have a relationship with the planet, that this is our communal home, and that it is part of who we are because the self is more than the skin, then there is an incredible opportunity for change and cultural evolution. The health of our planet is, at bottom, a moral issue.

Along with Richie Davidson, Alicia Lieberman, and Andrew Meltzoff, I was recently invited by the Dalai Lama to speak about compassion.[15] In my talk, I mentioned two studies that are causes for concern: mortality salience studies and empathy studies. Mortality salience studies look at what happens to us when we feel threatened, even subliminally (as we are now with terrorism). The studies show that people who feel under threat amplify who they consider in the ingroup and who they consider in the outgroup. They also treat ingroup people with more tenderness, kindness, and protection whereas they treat people in the outgroup with more hostility and disregard and disrespect. The other study shows that if you place a person in a scanner and you show them a facial expression, these little prefrontal areas light up for empathy. If you explain that this is a Dartmouth graduate, where the study was done, and he got a job at a new Internet company and he loves listening to music on his iPod, then the area for empathy lights up a lot. But if you explain that this is a guy who grew up in Korea, dropped out of school, and plays with Barbie dolls while listening to classical music, then this area does not light up at all even though it is the same face. If you identify someone as *not* similar to you, the circuitry of compassion and empathy shuts off. This is cause for concern because we live in a world full of threat, which increases the ingroup/outgroup distinction, and now we also know that when someone is in the outgroup, the person may not be seen as a human being.

The Dalai Lama's response probably surprised many because this was a religious meeting. He said the world's religions (whether Buddhism or Christianity or Judaism or Hinduism, any of the world's religions) have not persuasively addressed those issues, and it is unlikely that they ever will. So he argues for an ethic beyond religion that would promote more compassion.[16] Well, this was my suggestion: make the ethic about health. Every religious and nonreligious group could gather around the moral imperative that everyone on the planet, maybe even the whole planet, deserves health. And, if you look at the fundamental nature of health, it involves an expansion of the sense of self that you'll see derives from something damaged and lost in Barbara.

15. Seeds of Compassion Gathering, online: www.seedsofcompassion.org/.
16. See Dalai Lama and Norman, *Beyond Religion*.

Putting It Together: Brain, Relationships, and Mind

So how do we make sense of Barbara's story? The image of a triangle expresses for me what happened with Leanne and Barbara, and it says something broader too about what it means to be human.

Something had happened to Barbara's brain—illustrated by the three points of a triangle—that made the whole family collapse. As we have three sides to a triangle, we have three qualities to consider about being human. First, we have the embodied brain, which is the mechanism of energy and information flow. Second, we have relationships, which I define as the sharing of the energy and information flow. And finally we have mind, which I have yet to talk about and to define.[17] The definition of a relationship is when we share energy and information flow, where we resonate with it and with each other. When that happens, you literally feel what I feel. That's not just a poetic way of speaking; it is neurological.

The Role of Mirror Neurons and Resonating

Let me expand on what I mean when I say that feeling felt is neurological. In the early '90s, researchers in Parma, Italy, discovered a class of neurons that they called mirror neurons.[18] They were initially discovered in macaque monkeys but shown also to exist in human beings about ten years or so later. The evidence was at first indirect, but then a study at UCLA allowed open-skull surgery on a human being where surgeons actually found not only mirror-neuron properties but mirror-neuron activity in single neurons in a living human brain.

Your brain has circuits that are watching for patterns of actions in the world. When they are predictable, they start having a sensory implication of motor action. Imagine me looking around and maybe moving my hands about here and there. In this scenario, your sensory implication of motor action circuit (SIMA) cannot predict what I am going to do next because I

17. According to physicists, energy is the capacity to do stuff, and information is a pattern, such as a swirl, of energy. If I say, "Golden Gate Bridge," it takes energy to produce the sounds of those words, and the sound has a pattern to it that you can identify. If I say, "ga-ga-ga-ga," it may take just as much energy for me to make these sounds, but the pattern is not as rich or as easily identifiable, and there is not that much information there.

18. See Iacoboni, *Mirroring People*.

have no idea what I am doing. There is no identifiable pattern to my behavior, and so there is no sensory implication of what I am doing.

Now, imagine me lifting a bottle of water with my hand. As you see me do this, you figure out that I'm probably going to drink from the bottle. Your SIMA processing of what I am doing makes a map of basic motion and imbeds it in a map of my intention.[19] The ability to predict sequences allows us to map intention. Your SIMA processing also get you ready to do the same thing. We call that behavioral imitation. Finally, they do something called internal simulation. You feel thirsty, so you can imagine that Dan was thirsty and that this is why he drank.

This is what mirror neurons give us the capacity to do. I call it resonating with another human being. To put it in more direct terms, you feel what I feel. A patient of mine once said that she felt *felt*. Feeling felt is the first step toward healing in any psychotherapy. In fact, feeling felt is the first step toward healing in any kind of relationship.

Defining the Mind and Mindsight

What is the mind?[20] For about twenty years now, I have been busy contributing to a field called Interpersonal Neurobiology. Interpersonal Neurobiology is a consilient field, which invites every discipline of science into conversation about the nature of what it means to be human. We have also started involving people in the contemplative and religious communities, people in the arts and music, and people in education. We are a home of deep, far-reaching exploration into what makes up the mind and mental health. What are they, and how can we promote more kindness and compassion in the world?[21] This is a conversation that we have to have as a

19. Human beings are deeply social, and this is just some of the science behind our sociality.

20. When I speak to therapists, I usually do a fun little survey. So far, I have 98,650 mental health professionals that I have polled now. I will stop when I get to one hundred thousand. Interestingly, I've done this as well with educators and colleagues who are researchers, and I get the same response from them. My question is, how many of you have been given one lecture, even one lecture that defined—not described, but defined—what the mind is? It is about 2 to 5 percent. This is everywhere on this planet and in every discipline of mental health: psychiatry, psychology, social work, nursing, occupational therapy, and family therapy.

21. If this is of any interest to you, please come join us at www.drdansiegel.com/.

human family about the nature of the self and the ways in which we can strengthen the mind to get out of the delusion of our separateness.

How might we define the mind? The mind is an embodied, relational, and emergent process that regulates the flow of energy and information. It is embodied, meaning it is throughout the whole body. It is relational, meaning it is not just defined by the skin. It is also an emergent process, meaning it is part of a system that has the capacity to self-organize. And finally it is a process that gives you the ability to regulate the energy and information flow. Regulation entails two things: when you regulate a car, you have to monitor where you're going, and you have to modify the steering wheel and press on the accelerator or the brakes in order to stay on the road.

Mindsight is the ability to see energy and information flow in your relationships and in your body and in other people's bodies. So mindsight is the ability to perceive energy and information flow wherever it is happening. And it turns out that whether you're a parent, or a teacher with a student, like here at the university, or a therapist, a clinician with a client, or a patient, you can teach people to monitor with more depth and clarity so that energy and information flow in relationships and in the body (one's own body and other people's bodies) is more stable, has more clarity, and has more depth, richness, and detail. That's what we mean by teaching people to monitor.

If you had a camera that was jumping up and down, what would the result be of the video that you would get? A safe bet is that it would be blurry. We are finding that many of us do not have training in stabilizing attention, especially with the bewildering digital devices and technologies that we have today. We did a pilot study at UCLA showing that we can take people with attention-deficit problems and teach them to do mindfulness meditation.[22] The result was that we could get more improvements in their ability to stabilize attention than they would get with Ritalin. When we showed the results to our pharmacology colleagues at the university, their response was, "Which medication, and what dose was that?" We said, "Meditation, not medication." What the study shows is that you can teach people to regulate—to monitor and to modify—their energy information flow.

I want to emphasize that young children can learn these mindsight skills. The fact is that we teach our children to see the mind by the nonverbal ways we resonate with them from the very beginning of life. We then use words to describe things like thoughts and feelings, memories,

22. See online: www.marc.ucla.edu/. (MARC stands for Mindful Awareness Research Center.)

perceptions, attitudes, intentions—all the stuff that is the mental life that we have. We use words—words in addition to the nonverbal communication to describe that. I say, "We use words," but deaf children raised by parents who sign in a sophisticated way come up with mindsight equally well. The aspects are similar: the ability to see the mind and to be aware of the life of the mind which is the internal subjective life that each of us has. It shows that talking about the mind as well as nonverbal resonating about the mind are both important for the development of mindsight in children.

Regulation, Integration, and Spirituality

I want to suggest that spirituality is about energy and information flow. If we understand it that way, it would take the field of spirituality and the fields of psychology and attachment into a whole different realm. My hope is that this will allow us to have open, collaborative dialogue among the disciplines and sciences. When I spoke at my first spirituality conference, I had a two-hour talk, and I spent an hour of it going around the room getting definitions from participants. Almost every single participant said slightly different versions of the following two things: spirituality is feeling connected to a larger whole than just me, and finding a deeper meaning in life. I think those two are related.

John O'Donohue, one of my closest friends, who died four years ago, was a Catholic priest, a poet, a mystic, and a philosopher. He was also an unbelievable rogue, an incredible rascal of a guy, and just a beautiful man. We were writing a book about poetry and the brain, but he died very un-expectedly. Since he died, I know from direct experience that the energy and information flow that was the pattern that he created through his writ-ings, teachings, and his love and relationships continues on to this day even though his body is gone. If you want to call that his soul, then I'd be fine with that. If the system is energy and information flow, and patterns of energy and information are the essence of who someone is, and it is not limited to the skin, then yes we can talk about a soul.

Recall that in Barbara's case, the prefrontal cortex was damaged. The prefrontal cortex is a very important part of the brain because it connects everything to everything else. It connects the cortex to the limbic area and to the brainstem. It brings up data from the body and it is making maps of the signals from other parts of the nervous system. The differentiated parts are linked together, physically and functionally, to create those nine functions that we have been talking about. In fact, the central role of the middle prefrontal cortex is to do exactly that: it is literally linking differentiated areas together. To say it differently, the central role of the middle prefrontal cortex is integration, where integration is defined as the linkage of differentiated parts.

One day I had Barbara and her husband alone with me in the room. The kids were in the waiting room. I said, "Barbara, I need to ask you a question: what is life like for you since the accident?" There was silence for a moment, and then she looked at me with this flat face and said "well, I guess if I had to put a word to it, I guess I would say I have lost my soul." This was exactly what Leanne could not articulate and why she had stopped speaking. However you interpret the word soul, from a religious point of view or an essence point of view, Barbara had lost who she was. This embodied brain, these relationships she could have, and the mind that emerged as a process of her relationships and her body, were no longer able to do something very important.

Conclusion: Integration, Health, and Spiritual Connection

I want you to consider the concept of integration. If you look at the mathematics of complex systems, you will discover that they are open, self-organizing systems capable of chaotic behavior. A key feature is that the self-organization is emergent, and differentiation among the parts is maintained. If differentiation disappears, it would no longer be a complex system. It would not be a healthy relationship either. If, on the other hand, everybody ignored each other, there would be no linkage. Secure attachment comes from integration. In fact, you can reinterpret the entire field of attachment through this lens of integration, and in doing so you can make deep sense of the neural as well as the relational implications of attachment.

Complex systems move in an optimal way, which is called maximizing complexity, by linking differentiated parts. It is what you do when you sing in harmony. You are differentiating your voices and you are linking them. Here is the thing that I find amazing: the vitality that emerges is contagious. It's fantastic. I picture it as a flowing river—a river of integration. But when a system is not moving toward an integrated harmony, it goes either to chaos or to rigidity. Chaos and rigidity are what result from impaired integration.

In the early '90s when I read this sitting at my desk, I jumped up and I grabbed the diagnostic and statistical manual of disorders (DSM). I realized that every single disorder, every symptom of every syndrome in that book, is an example of chaos, rigidity, or both. In those days, it was just a hypothesis that I had. Now, however, we know that trauma and neglect destroy and block the growth of integrated fibers of the brain.[23] Just recently Marcus Raichel showed that when the resting brain is integrated there is health.[24] When it is not integrated, you get schizophrenia, autism, bipolar disorder, and obsessive-compulsive disorders. So now there is support for the hypothesis that an integrated mind is a healthy mind, which is what I presented to the Dalai Lama: the idea that integration is health. When you are not in health, whether you're a community or a family, or a romantic relationship or just living in your body, you are not integrated, and there is either chaos or rigidity or both. So this triangle is a triangle of well-being and resilience.

We are now in a position to say—and this is true whether you look at attachment research or look at couples' relationships or just examine the way the brain develops over the lifespan—that we need each other not just to be there but actually to be resonating with the other person. What we really need is to feel felt. It is this ability to sense the internal world of another person. I want to suggest to you that when energy and information flow are resonating, it stimulates the growth and maintains the vital life of integration in the nervous system, in the whole body, and in our relationships. The ultimate outcome of that is not only a sense of health but a sense of deep spiritual connection.

Christian's Response

It is often the case that our tragedies tell us more about who we are than our successes or our victories. It is an insight that the Homeric tradition in which Plato and Aristotle worked never was quite able to bring on board. It stands in great contrast to the Hebraic tradition, which is much more sensitive to the ways human life can and often does go wrong. It comes, I think, from the deep memory of having been enslaved and exiled. You find the same sensibility in the music, theology, and philosophy of the African American tradition. The blue note is a true and human note. And the tragic story of Barbara and Leanne reveals something about us that is true to our humanity, namely, that the self is more like a plural verb than a singular noun.

23. Teicher et al., "Childhood Neglect Is Associated with Reduced Corpus Callosum Area." See also Siegel, *The Developing Mind*, 119.

24. Zhang and Raichle, "Disease and the Brain's Dark Energy."

As I listen to Dan Siegel give his understanding of the human being, I am aware of something that strikes me as quite remarkable. My inner voice and self-talk says "yes, that's me," or, "I've done that." I'm not alienated from my sense of self by the science, but rather I feel as if I'm being reintroduced to myself. I can extend a compassion that comes from understanding what is going on inside without the sense of being released from the responsibility of being a person in relationship. This feature of being able to understand but not excuse seems to me to be of crucial importance in situations in which a no! needs to be said.

What Dan has achieved, then, is to hold together neuroscience, attachment theory, and a conception of a healthy mind in such a way that they deepen lived experience. The brilliance of it is easily missed. It seems simple to say that the mind is an emergent process, which regulates the flow of energy and information between the interior and exterior environment (it is embodied and relational). Or, for example, to say that an integrated mind is a healthy mind (where integration is understood as the linking of differentiated parts).

It may be simple, but notice what you can do with it! Now you have a definition of health as the homeostatic and harmonic river-like flow of integration between chaos and rigidity. You don't have to tell Mennonites twice that harmony is healthy and good for us. We know that already, and we know it in our bones. We also know that it is not good for us when a voice is not heard. I want to stress that this is not primarily cognitive but embodied and emotional. The connection and the flow of energy come, not when you feel understood, but when you feel felt. Here the river of integration becomes a river of healing.

One of the intellectual difficulties with this book is that it has the term *spirituality* in the title. *Spirituality* gets used in so many different ways that it is unclear what it means. I want to suggest that we use Dan's definition of integration as the linking of differentiated parts, and that we expand it such that when we are talking about spirituality, we are talking about making contact or linking with that which is bigger.

In a remarkable passage at the very end of Revelation (chapter 22), John sees a new city descending. An angel shows him the river of the water of life, sparkling like crystal and flowing from the throne of God. On either side of the river stands a tree of life, and the leaves of the tree, explains John, are for the healing of the nations. To me, John's vision of a river of life and healing of the nations is about as big as it gets. The whole of the New Testament ends with one final invitation: Let the thirsty come!

3

From Me to We

Embracing Membership in a Larger Whole

Daniel Siegel

An Interpersonal Neurobiology View of Attachment Theory

WHEN JOHN BOWLBY AND Mary Ainsworth, who were the founders of attachment theory and research, developed their protocols, we did not know much about the relationship between attachment and the brain. As it turns out, eight of the nine prefrontal functions, which Barbara lost when her brain was damaged, happen also to be proven outcomes of what secure attachment creates. I think it is an amazing finding that the search to explain Barbara's loss of soul and Leanne's response to it led to the same list of functions (except one).[1] I have come to believe that it is not a coincidence. They share something important: integration. The prefrontal cortex is an integrative area of the embodied brain, and attachment relationships can be understood as examples of integrated social systems of energy and information flow.

This is an Interpersonal Neurobiology view of attachment. On this view, secure attachment is an example of a relationship that promotes integration. For a relationship to be integrative, you have to honor differences— even thrive in the differences. I am thinking of a community that honors the different opinions people have, or a parent who honors the difference

1. The ninth function, intuition, has never been looked at by people studying attachment. I'm not saying that intuition is not an outcome of secure attachment. I'm saying that such has not yet been shown because it has not yet been studied.

between the child's temperamental features and the parent's expectations. Linkage is a way to name compassionate, loving, resonant communication and connection between and among differentiated parts. The entire field of attachment can be gathered up with one word: *integration*.

John Bowlby, who was a clinician and a psychoanalyst, proposed the idea that it was not the fantasies that children have but the actual experiences that were important to their inner organization. At the time, this was a radical idea, and it was quickly rejected by colleagues as heresy. In spite of criticism from peers, he claimed that the actual lived experience of children shapes what he called a model of security that children carry inside of them, and which impacts their ability to navigate life.[2] This internal working model of security goes forward with them, and it is continually modified as the child develops. If you have suboptimal attachment, then you face many more challenges growing up.

The Strange Situation

Mary Ainsworth came as a colleague to study with Bowlby. She developed a research protocol called the strange situation, in which you study a parent-child dyad in the first year of life and then bring them into a laboratory setting. The infant strange-situation protocol runs as follows: The parent is with the baby in the room. A stranger comes in, and the parent leaves for three minutes while the stranger stays with the baby. The parent returns to the room. The stranger leaves, and later the parent also leaves the room so the baby is alone in the room. Then, after three minutes, the parent returns. All this is filmed. The infant strange situation is a separation paradigm, but what is measured is the behavior of the baby at the time of reunion (reunion behavior). Ainsworth found that what was recorded in over seventy hours of direct observation of the parent–child dyad in the first year of life correlates well with the results of the strange situation.

Initially, researchers found three categories of responses. Ultimately a fourth category was added by Mary Main, one of Mary Ainsworth's students. She along with Erik Hesse have developed a deep study of things discussed below.[3]

2. For a comprehensive history and review of attachment research, see Cassidy and Shaver, *The Handbook of Attachment*.

3. See Sroufe and Siegel, *The Verdict Is In*; and Wylie and Turner, *The Attuned Therapist*.

Securely attached children have parents during the first year of life who are responsive and consistent in their caregiving. Let's make the baby a boy and the parent a mom, just so we have the *he* and *she* clear. During the infant strange situation, when the mother returns to the room, the baby responds by being happy and touching base with the mother (proximity seeking). He has had a year of responsive, consistent caregiving, and there are a bunch of new toys in the room, so he quickly goes back to playing with the toys. Sixty to sixty-five percent of the nonclinical population demonstrate secure attachment. These children go on to meet their intellectual potential, have good relationships with other people, can balance their emotions well, have the ability to see the mind clearly, and have a coherent narrative about their lives.

The next grouping, about 20 percent of the nonclinical population, have an avoidant attachment with their primary caregiver.[4] The avoidantly attached child has experienced a year of distant and rejecting interaction with a parent who does not see their nonverbal signals. After the avoidantly attached child is placed in the infant strange situation, what will the reunion behavior look like when the mother returns? Outwardly, the child will ignore the return of mom because after a year of a disconnected way of being, the child has learned that trying to connect to mom does not work. Inwardly, however, the child is stressed out. He knows mom is important, but he has learned to minimize attachment behavior. He gets stressed (his skin gets sweaty), avoids mom, and continues to play with the toys. These kids are experienced by their peers in school as controlling and not very nice.[5] My experience as a clinician is that when they become adults, they are disconnected from their own internal mental life, they do not know what they feel, and they are not in touch with their bodies. They also do not remember their childhoods.

About 10–15 percent of the nonclinical population has an ambivalent attachment. In the first year of life, instead of being attuned and consistent, there was inconsistency and sometimes even intrusive behavior on the part of the parent. Imagine being that child in the room. Mom leaves, or it could be Dad—let's do a dad this time and have the baby be a girl. When Dad returns, what will her reunion behavior be like? The attachment system is about feeling secure and feeling seen. What is her response after a year of

4. You never say that the baby is avoidant. Instead, you say that the attachment is avoidant or the relationship is avoidant, because the baby can have an avoidant attachment with Dad but a secure attachment with Mom. Attachment is based on the actual experiences that a child has with caregivers. This is why attachment is not related to temperament. One child with a particular temperament can have two different attachments.

5. See Wylie and Turner, *The Attuned Therapist.*

inconsistently feeling secure and feeling intruded upon? Unlike the avoidantly attached child, who responds by a damping down of the attachment system, she ramps the attachment system up. She gets revved up. Will he be here or not? Will I be okay or not? Because the child does not know, there is uncertainty, ambivalence, and confusion, which feels like an inner sense of dread. She responds by clinging to the parent because Dad is here right now, and if I grab onto him tight enough, then maybe it will all be okay. Unlike the disconnected internal working model of the avoidantly attached child, here you see an internal sense of confusion and dread.

In addition to these three categories, Mary Main found a fourth that overlaps with the others.[6] When you are given this fourth category of disorganized, you are also given a secondary classification of either secure, avoidant, or ambivalent attachment. In a nonclinical population, you see anywhere from 10 to 15 percent and in a clinical population, upwards of 70–75 percent. Main and Hesse postulated that the child has experienced terrifying or in other ways confusing experiences from the caregiver. Why would that be a different sort of problem than inconsistency? Well, the reason is there are two circuits in the brain: one is the circuit of safety, and the other is the circuit of attachment. With the circuit of safety, if your brain assesses that you are being threatened, your three-hundred-million-year-old circuit of safety says, I have to get away from this source of danger. At the same time, however your two-hundred-million-year-old circuit of attachment says, I'm in a state of terror, and I should go to the attachment figure (your dad in this case). So you have a two-hundred-million-year-old circuit that says, Go towards Dad, and you have a three-hundred-million-year-old circuit that says, Get away from Dad. How can you solve that problem? You cannot. It is an unsolvable biological paradox. Disorganized attachment is a uniquely dis-integrating attachment.[7]

Let me briefly review the categories of attachment. Children with secure attachment have had parents who were consistent and connecting, and they have an integrated state. Avoidantly attached kids are disconnected, and they try to go it alone. Ambivalently attached kids are confused inside: they feel uncertain, and the kids in school with them think they are insecure. Those are all organized strategies of attachment and they are very different from the disorganized group, which has the most severe psychopathology. Disorganizedly attached kids have trouble regulating

6. This can be a bit confusing because the numbers no longer add up to 100 percent.

7. I am using *integration* in the technical sense of linking differentiated parts.

their emotions, and they cannot think clearly under stress. They fragment consciousness in a process called dissociation, and they have severely disrupted relationships. If you want to do preventative work, you could take every child with disorganized attachment and at least move them toward ambivalent or avoidant models of attachment, and you would be doing a big service in the world.

Before we move on, I want to comment on reactive attachment disorder. If a child is raised in an orphanage and has no attachment figures, it's very different from the categories we've discussed so far. The lack of attachment leads to serious problems with the capacity to have and hold onto intimate relationships. The four categories you see here are forms of insecure attachment. Reactive attachment disorder is not an example of insecure attachment. It is a disorder of attachment because of the lack of an attachment figure. People sometimes ask me, which one is reactive attachment? The answer is, none of them. It is a whole different experience to have no attachment figure—different even from having one who is terrifying.

Adult Attachment Interview

Mary Main was able to find that the best predictor of the security of attachment for a child is the way a parent has made sense of his or her own life. I think this is the most amazing discovery in all of psychology in the last one hundred years, and yet hardly anyone knows about it. Mary Main discovered that you can interview parents, even in pregnant couples, and predict what the unborn child's attachment will be to each of those parents. This is based on the results of the adult-attachment interview (AAI) alone.

Mary Main just recently agreed to release the AAI to clinicians. It was an amazing moment because many of us have been asking for this for twenty years. Over the years, researchers have studied more than twenty thousand interviews. The conclusion is that the narrative of the parent in the AAI is highly predictive of what the child's attachment will be—even more predictive than direct observation.[8]

The interview asks how you remember your own childhood, and how you make sense of how your childhood has impacted you. With a child who is securely attached, those parents have a flexible, coherent, self-reflective, balanced perspective.[9] If you have had an avoidant attachment, however, it

8. It is 75 percent accurate, which is impressive in psychology.

9. For a step-by-step walk through developing a coherent narrative, see Siegel,

is very likely that the parent who is disconnected to you has what is called a dismissing narrative. They insist that relationships do not matter and dismiss their importance. They are incoherent in the sense that they say, "I don't remember my childhood, but I know my childhood didn't affect me." You cannot have both of those: If you do not remember your childhood, then you cannot know whether or how your childhood affected you. The state of mind of dismissive attachment is also inflexible in the apparent lack of openness on reflecting on one's own autobiographical story.[10]

If you are a child with an anxious attachment, it is very likely that your parent had a preoccupied narrative. Unlike the dismisser, this one is filled with recollections of childhood. They cannot stop thinking about it, and there is an intrusiveness in the way the narrative comes out.

Finally, the narrative outcome for disorganizedly attached kids is unresolved trauma or grief. At the moment in the narrative when we are asking questions such as, who did you lose in your childhood?, or, were you ever terrified in your childhood?, the speaker gets disoriented. This is the only research instrument of which I'm aware that has a systematic way of assessing not only if someone's been traumatized but also if that trauma or loss is unresolved. The research clearly shows that if you have been traumatized or had a severe loss in your childhood, and you have resolved it, then your children will do fine. So the distinction between lack of resolution versus resolution is absolutely essential, and it often gets overlooked or ignored, but not, as I said, in the AAI.

The narrative finding is so much more predictive than direct observation because it allows us to understand the inner workings of the brain of the parent and the ways in which non-integrated internal and interpersonal states shape attachment.[11] The narrative findings offer us a window into what may be happening in the brain of someone with unresolved trauma or loss. It also shows how the process of psychotherapy can

Mindsight; and Siegel, *The Mindful Therapist.* All of this information can be found in *Mindsight* and *The Developing Mind.* For suggestions about how to incorporate this into parenting, see Siegel and Hartzell, *Parenting from the Inside Out.* Training DVDs are available at the Mindsight Institute website: http://www.mindsightinstitute.com/.

10. I should say that there is something called childhood amnesia. No one can remember much before the ages of five to seven. We are talking about people that do not remember what happened between the ages of nine and fifteen, and especially relational things. They can remember sporting events and who was the president and what car their family was driving, but they cannot remember relational experiences.

11. I wrote *The Developing Mind* to provide a neurobiological explanation of this profound finding in attachment research.

move the brain from lack of resolution of trauma and loss to resolution. Psychotherapy does so by linking differentiated parts to each other, moving from a lack of integration to integration, and consequently also moving from no resolution to resolution of trauma and loss.

Flipping Your Lid: An Example of Disintegration

An integrated brain is one in which input from various parts are linked together: the social with the bodily, the somatic with the brain stem, and the limbic with the cortical. Input from all those parts is brought together as a coordinated and balanced whole by the prefrontal region such that it becomes a functional whole. Recall now the list of functions for which the prefrontal cortex is central: body regulation, attuned communication, emotional balance, response flexibility, fear modulation, insight, empathy, morality, and intuition.

Have you ever been in a situation in which you temporarily lost maybe one, two, or possibly all those functions? I call it "flipping your lid." I was a research fellow with the National Institute of Mental Health (NIMH), studying attachment. I had our newborn with me, and I flipped my lid. I thought to myself, "You are insane. You're a board-certified child psychiatrist. You're a research fellow in attachment. And, you're a nut. What's wrong with you?" Around that time, I met Leanne.[12] I learned from Barbara's case that you do not have to have a horrible car accident to get your middle prefrontal cortex temporarily not to function.

I started teaching my patients that they could have a temporarily dysfunctional/disintegrated system. I already knew from personal experience that parents were vulnerable to disintegration, but I came to discover that many parents had been hiding their ruptured connections with their children in shame because of what people might think of them. Trauma survivors are especially vulnerable to flipping their lids. They go there more rapidly, they stay down longer, and it is harder for them to repair when they come out of it. But the truth is that we are all vulnerable to disintegration.

About ten years ago or so, Mary Hartzell and I started teaching together doing seminars and workshops for teachers, parents, and kids.[13] The morning after I had talked about our vulnerability to flipping our lids, a

12 See chapter 2, above.

13. We ultimately gathered the material in *Parenting from the Inside Out.*

mom comes up to me and she says, "Dan, I have to tell you something. You know the flipping the lid thing you taught me last night?"

I said, "Yeah."

She started to cry. She said, "You can't understand what it meant to me to learn that."

I said, "What did it mean?"

She said, "Instead of beating up on myself, I said to myself, this is not your fault, but it is your responsibility. Instead of hiding in shame, I could go this morning to my daughter and say, 'Anna, I'm so sorry. That must have been so scary for you.'"

Her daughter started crying, and they repaired. You can always repair if you take yourself back to reconnect and by owning what you did. Sadly, people flip their lids, and then they say, "Oh, no, that wasn't me," or they forget it, or they justify it by saying, "Oh, my kid really deserved that."

If your child experiences you flipping your lid, and there is no repair because of feelings of shame or denial or whatever on the part of the parent, then there can be serious consequences for the child. What is amazing to me, however, is that teaching people about the brain invites them to become more compassionate with themselves and with others. It helps them get to a place where they can own their actions and go back to repair. Ever since that encounter ten years ago when a mother told me how important it had been for her to learn how brains work, I have learned that people need to know how their brains are a part of their lives. Flipping your lid is just one example.

The Wheel of Awareness

What can you do besides good therapy? What can you do to help grow these areas of the brain? How do you work at integration? Where does mindfulness fit into all this? Mary Hartzell and I put in the word *mindfulness* in our book, by which we meant being conscientious, caring, and intentional in what you do.[14] We were surprised when we were told that there was a whole field called mindfulness meditation, which we did not know much about, but which I have subsequently come to recognize as very important especially as it relates to integration.

14. See Siegel and Hartzell, *Parenting from the Inside Out.*

I will walk you through what Jon Kabat-Zinn calls a mindfulness meditation. I designed this as an integrative meditation.[15] Using the image of a wheel, the center of the wheel is the hub, the outer circle of the wheel is the rim, and spokes connect the hub to the rim. A spoke represents the experience of awareness, and anything of which you are aware is on the rim. The wheel differentiates the architecture of consciousness. We will link these elements that are differentiated from each other in the practice we are about to do and thereby connect the wheel. The idea is to integrate consciousness. With the five senses, you bring the outside world in. The sixth sense is a sense of the interior of the body.

This is an internal reflective practice, not a relaxation technique. It requires that you be very active in your body. It is helpful to put two feet flat on the floor, have your legs uncrossed, and sit up straight. You should be comfortable but have a sense of purpose. You are going to be focusing on mental experiences. For some people, that is very engaging. For others, that is very boring, and when people get bored, they fall asleep. Part of your task is to keep yourself awake. Even though you may want to do this with your eyes closed, you can keep your eyes open and you can do this entire practice standing up if you need.

We will begin the exercise with a very brief breath-awareness practice. With your eyes open, let your attention come to the middle of the room. Send your attention back to the far wall. Bring your attention back to the middle of the room. Notice how you can determine where your attention goes. Let your attention come to a book-reading distance, so it is really close to you. Let your attention find your breathing and begin at the level of the nostrils with the sensation of air as it comes in and goes out. Notice that you can let your attention move to the level of the chest as it rises and falls, and notice you can bring your attention down to the level of the abdomen. Place a hand on your belly and notice that when the air fills the lungs, the belly moves outward and when the air escapes the lungs, the belly moves inward. Let the outward and inward movement of the abdomen be the focus of attention, and take a moment now to focus on the breath moving in and out.

Let me share with you an ancient story that's been passed down through the generations. The mind is like the ocean; and deep in the ocean, beneath the surface, it is calm and clear. From this deep place beneath the

15. See Siegel, *The Mindful Therapist*; and Siegel, *Mindsight*. It is also available free to download to your iPod or mp3 player at dr.dansiegel.com/.

surface, it's possible to notice what's happening at the surface, whether it's flat or choppy or even a full storm. No matter what those surface conditions are, deep in the ocean, it's calm and clear. Sensing the breath brings you to the depths of the mind beneath the surface activity. From this deep place, you can notice mental activities as they rise and fall in awareness like brain waves at the surface of the mind—those emotions and thoughts, memories, and attitudes. You can be aware of all of this—the images, the beliefs, the mental activities—from the depths of your mind.

You can practice breath awareness at home for a few minutes every morning. You simply sense the breath, and when a mental activity distracts you, then lovingly and gently return your attention to the breath. Focus on the breath knowing that it brings you to this deep place in the mind. It can improve the health of your body, your mind, and even your relationships.

As you are focusing on the breath, let the image of the wheel of awareness come to mind. We'll now begin a review of the rim. The rim is divided into four parts. We will begin in the first segment, which is the part of the rim that represents the sensations that bring the outside world in. We will begin with the sense of hearing, letting sound fill awareness. Allow yourself to hear the sounds, and imagine a spoke sent out to the area of sound. Then, allow that spoke to move over a bit to the sense of sight and vision. If your eyes are closed, you can either let light come in through the closed eyelids or just gently open them, letting vision fill awareness now. We move the spoke over a bit more to the sense of smell, letting any scents and odors fill awareness, followed by the sense of taste. And now moving the spoke over one more time in this first sector to the sense of touch—anywhere where the skin is touching something—your clothing, skin touching skin.

Now taking a bit of a deeper breath, imagine moving the spoke over from this first segment of the rim to the next segment of the rim, which is the interior of the body. Let's begin with the facial area, sensing the muscles and bones of the face and then moving to the muscles and bones of the scalp and the back of the head, to the neck, and then the throat. Moving attention to the shoulders and then down both arms to the fingertips. And then bringing attention to the upper back and the chest and then the lower back and the abdomen and then moving to the hips and focusing attention down both legs to the toes. Now, move attention inwardly to the pelvic area, letting the genitals fill awareness and then bringing attention inwardly in the abdomen and the intestinal area. Now let awareness move up to the stomach region, and then to the interior of the throat, letting sensations fill awareness. Now, move your attention to the interior of the lungs and then center attention in the heart region. Broaden your attention to include the whole of the interior of the body, and take a bit of a deeper breath, knowing that the wisdom of the body is always available to you in this segment of the wheel's rim.

Imagine moving the spoke of the awareness wheel over to the next segment of the rim. This is the segment that represents our mental activities, our feelings and emotions, our thoughts, memories, images, attitudes, beliefs, intentions, hopes, and dreams. Anything that is a mental activity rests here in this segment of the rim. With our attention resting on this segment, the first part is to simply allow any kind of mental activity—thoughts, memories, feelings, or images—into the hub of the mind and see what that feels like for you.

For the second part, invite anything to come up from this aspect of the rim, noticing how a mental activity—a thought, a memory, or an image—first presents itself to awareness. Is it sudden? Is it gradual? How does that happen? Once it presents itself to awareness, how does it stay present? Is it pulsing? Is it constant? How does it actually stay present in awareness? How does it leave awareness? Is it just replaced by another mental activity? Or is there a gap between two mental activities? If there is a gap, what does that gap feel like? You are going to study the architecture of your own mental life by studying how things enter, stay present, and exit awareness. Take a deeper breath as we let this segment of the rim that represents mental activities go.

Imagine moving the spoke over one more time to our final aspect of the rim of the awareness wheel. This segment of the rim represents our sense of connection to other people, other things outside the body—our sense of interconnectedness with other entities. Let yourself become aware of your sense of connection to people in this room sitting physically close to you right here and now. Let that sense of connection expand outward to people who are filling this room and sharing this experience right here together. Let it expand to a sense of connection to family and friends not in this room, to people who live within your community, and people at your work or at school. Expand this further to all people who live in your city, to a sense of connection to all people who live here in your state with you. Expand that out to people who live in your country, whichever country that is. Let that move out to all human beings who share our common home, this planet we call Earth. Let that sense of connection expand even further to all living beings on the planet.

Science is beginning to demonstrate what wisdom traditions through-out the world have known for thousands of years, which is that giving love and kindness—practicing love and compassion—brings health into the interior world and into the social world. It brings wisdom and well-being into the entire system of life in which we live. Send out wishes of love and compassion to the world of all living beings, and then bring those wishes of compassion and love back to our interior world, the world that begins inside the body but that we are learning does not end there. Bring it back to these bodies that walk the planet. Bring love and kindness toward ourselves.

This would be a place to end the wheel-of-awareness practice by fo-cusing on the breath, but there is one more step that we can do while we are on this journey together. Focusing on your breath moving in and out, bring the hub of the wheel of awareness to mind. For this step, imagine sending the spoke out from the hub. Instead of that spoke going straight to the rim, curve it around and bend the spoke back to the hub. You are focusing a beam of attention from the hub onto the hub itself. Experience what awareness of awareness feels like. I invite you to find the breath one more time, riding the wave of the inbreath and the outbreath. Knowing that sensing the breath brings you to that open, clear state of the hub of the mind. I invite you now to take a deeper, more intentional breath as we bring this wheel-of-awareness practice to a close. Let your eyes gently open, and we will return to our discussion.

The Plane of Possibility

What are we doing when we are sensing the *awareness of awareness*? Recall that one aspect of the mind is that it is an emergent process that regulates energy and information flow. If that is true, then the science that we need to describe this place of the awareness of awareness is quantum mechanics.

In quantum mechanics, energy flows like a wave, connecting events across distances. When you drop a rock in a pond, for example, two frogs on either end of the pond would have their lily pads go up and down at the same time. A single wave is happening in two places at once. This can seem strange, but when you realize that energy flows in waves, then it doesn't seem so strange. Still, it gets people nervous. But have you ever had the experience of knowing what someone else was thinking miles away? It hap-pens when you are connected to somebody. It happens to me with my wife. She is probably thinking about calling me right now because I just said that.

In quantum mechanics, the act of observation or the act of being aware influences the movement of the energy you are observing. The fabric of quantum reality is incredibly sensitive to consciousness such that awareness shapes the movement of energy. In quantum mechanics, nothing is certain. It is all degrees of probability. Notice that if the degree of probability is near zero, then anything is possible.[16]

How does this relate to experience? Well, let's say you are in a hungry mood, and you say to yourself, "I'm hungry." You are at what we can view as an elevated "plateau" representing an increased probability, because what you will do next is predetermined, and your degree of probability for your action has gone up from near zero. You've moved from the plane to a plateau, in this case of hunger. I am likely going to eat soon because I'm hungry. I realize that I want Ethiopian food. It is now almost certain that I will be eating lunch at the Blue Nile on South Main Street. Maybe you and I are both having lunch at the Blue Nile because you are hungry too. We are at a peak of probability. Peaks are important. You have to eat, pay taxes, and press on the brakes at a stop sign. When we go back down to a plateau, possibilities begin to open up but only somewhat. I might instead have wanted Indian food, but I was going to eat soon either way.

Our lives are filled with peaks and plateaus that don't move to the open plane of possibility. When you are in the plane of possibility, anything is possible. Because we are filled with thoughts and ideas of this and that, we rarely bring ourselves down to this open plane. I want to suggest to you that the hub in the wheel of awareness represents this open plane of possibility. Awareness arises from this open plane of possibility. We experience it as the hub of the mind. But anything that's outside of the hub is a various degree of certainty when you're all the way out at a thought. That is a certain thought, and they come and go. What you experience in the exercise of being aware is that you are moving from an observational place in the open plane to various plateaus and peaks. Integration of consciousness loosens up rigid peaks and incessant plateaus so that you can go back and forth with ease.

The model suggests that what makes us different from each other are our plateaus and peaks. They are unique for each of us and they change over our lifespan. But the place that is the same for all of us is the open plane of possibility. We all share it. Your plane and my plane are the same open plane. We are just manifestations of different plateaus and peaks. So this

16. For a graph that pictures this aspect of quantum mechanics, see Siegel, *The Mindful Therapist*.

exercise of the wheel of awareness and noticing the awareness of awareness becomes a spiritual practice.

As I have been working with clients on what I call *transpirational integration*, which is a kind of final integration of integration, what happens in their lives—without their even trying—is that they will say, "For me to have meaning in my life, I've got to do something to help people, to empower poor people, to feed the hungry, to make a difference for others," or "I've got to work to prevent violence in this world." They begin to feel a part of something much larger, and there is deep meaning in this. In my experience, the two big things about spirituality are meaning and a sense of being connected to something much larger than what the skin is enclosing.

How can we define a spiritual mind? I would say that a spiritual mind is a mind that has access to the hub where you allow yourself to drop into yourself in the plane of possibility. You open your self up to the deep, deep reality that we are all manifestations of the same essence. The plane of possibility is where hope bubbles up, where compassion is born, and where our deep sense of attachment and connection to each other arises. We drop into the plane of possibility so that we can bring more love and compassion into this world. We bring this kind of spiritual practice, this deeply rooted openness to our interconnectedness into the world, not just for the time these bodies are here, but for generations ahead so that people living 150 years from now who come into this auditorium will have a better life and a better world because of everything you and I have all done together.

4

The Social Regulation of Emotion

JAMES A. COAN[1]

The Cheetahs of Emotion Regulation

WHAT DO WE DO when we feel strong emotions such as fear, anger, and sadness? We regulate our emotions. *Emotion regulation* is the way in which we cope with our strong feelings. Humans are very good at this. For example, we can do something that no other animal on earth can do: we can tell ourselves that "it's only a movie." I like to think of humans as the cheetahs of self-regulation because just as cheetahs are the fastest animals on earth, humans are the best emotion regulators on earth. We are able to tell ourselves "it's only a movie" by exercising our prefrontal cortex. Unlike most other animals, we have a very powerful prefrontal cortex indeed, but it is also very costly. If we have to tell ourselves "it's only a movie" for long periods of time, then we become exhausted and less able to regulate our behavior.

How do other animals regulate their emotions? Animals of all mammalian species regulate their emotions through social proximity and contact. They cannot tell themselves "it's only a movie" like we can, but a young chimpanzee can run over to his mother and cling to her when he's frightened. That will bring down his level of fear, and that's how many other animals regulate their emotions. It is a trick that animals have learned. Of course, the human animal does it too. We stay close to each other, we help each other out, and very frequently that manifests as a clasping of hands.

1. Department of Psychology, Gilmer Hall, PO Box 400400, Charlottesville, VA 22904. E-mail: jcoan@virginia.edu.

Hand-holding has been a major part of my research program, as I'll describe in a moment, but first I want to emphasize the importance of emotion regulation through social proximity for general health and human thriving.

There is a very famous graph in the sciences, which comes from *Science* magazine in 1988.[2] Along the *x* axis, the scale goes from low to high levels of social contact and integration (the higher up you go, the more social contact and integration you have). Along the *y* axis, the scale goes from low to high age-adjusted risk of death (the higher up you go, the more likely you are to die). The graph shows a startling series of negative correlations. In regions all over the world (across many different cultures and many different kinds of societies), the more socially isolated you are, the earlier you are likely to die. You might ask of what? The answer is, of anything and everything—from accidents to diseases.

Many years ago, when I first started doing research, I was working with John Gottman at the University of Washington. We observed the social regulation of emotion among couples who were fighting.[3] We brought couples into the laboratory and goaded them into fighting with each other. We found that within some couples, members were capable of soothing each other's physiology with kind and gentle words even in the midst of conflict. We also found that the degree to which members of a couple were capable of soothing each other corresponded to how well that couple's marriage was doing four years later. The couples best at soothing each other even amid conflict were the happiest couples. Those who were a little less skilled at regulating each other's physiology were less happy, and those even less skilled at regulating each other's physiology had divorced.

The point of these two illustrations is this: humans do engage in the social regulation of emotion, and our receptivity to regulation from other people as well as our ability to help others regulate their emotions have real consequences that impact how we live our lives.

We Return to Baseline

I want to describe a study that I did about five years ago. We brought couples into the laboratory, and we asked one member of that couple to go into an MRI scanner. I don't know if you've ever had an MRI. It is not a particularly

2. See House et al., "Social Relationships and Health."

3. See Gottman et al., "Predicting Marital Happiness and Stability from Newlywed Interactions."

pleasant experience, but that wasn't good enough for me. We actually put them under threat of mild electric shock because I needed to know how the brain responds when it is frightened. If we can figure *that* out, then we might know how people help each other under frightening conditions—how the brain turns a helping hand into feelings of security and confidence.

To frighten the brain we showed people either a red *x*, which indicated a 20 percent chance of electric shock, or a blue *o*, which indicated total safety (see Figure 4.1). We did this under three conditions: 1) while subjects were alone, 2) while subjects held the hand of a stranger they'd never met before, and 3) while subjects held the hand of their romantic partners. We looked first at how the brain responded to the threat of shock when people were alone, and then looked at how that changed across these hand-holding conditions. With this one condition—the alone condition—we are replicating many, many studies of threat response in the brain, and we wanted to make sure that we could see what everybody else was seeing first. Then we wanted to see what changes occurred when we added social support.

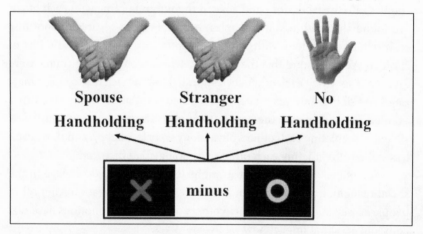

We contrasted a red *x*—indicating threat of shock—with a blue circle, indicating safety, under three counterbalanced conditions: Spouse hand-holding, stranger hand-holding, and no hand-holding.

As part of the study, we have an unpleasantness rating. (No aspect of this condition is really pleasant.) We found that the experience of our shock experiment was least unpleasant when subjects were holding the hands of their partners. We found no difference between the alone condition and the stranger condition. We also asked how agitated the subjects' bodies felt, and here we saw what we call an "any hand" affect. Any hand, spouse or stranger, seemed to relax the body even though it didn't relax how unpleasant their experience felt to them. The story so far, at least in terms of lived experience, seems to be that hand-holding, whether with spouse or stranger, causes a mild decrease in the response to threat, and that holding a spouse's hand causes a *big* decrease in the response to threat.

But what about activity in the brain? When you're facing a threat of mild electric shock, your brain becomes very active doing all kinds of things. You perceive a bunch of problems that you need to solve. The interesting question then is, which regions of the brain, and which of these different problems, are impacted by hand-holding? Two regions of the threat -responsive brain in particular—the ventral anterior and posterior portions of the cingulate cortex—were less responsive to the threat cue when any hand-holding happened. This is interesting because these regions have to do with somatic arousal, which is your body's preparation for the potential threat. The decrease in activity is reflected in people's reports concerning the unpleasantness of the experience. Systems controlling bodily arousal seemed to be responsive to *any* kind of hand-holding. And in fact, when we look broadly in the brain, a number of brain regions associated with preparing the body for action seem to be a little less active during hand-holding, no matter whether the held hand belongs to stranger or partner.

Our participants also showed steep decreases in activity within the prefrontal cortex if they were holding their spouse's hand while being confronted with the threat of electric shock. Remember that the prefrontal cortex is what we use to tell ourselves "it's only a movie." For reasons that might be unclear initially, this decrease in brain activity surprised me— because when I first designed this experiment I thought that the pathway linking hand-holding to the down-regulation of emotional responding in the brain was going to run through the prefrontal cortex. If that were the case, however, then hand-holding would cause *increased* activity in the prefrontal cortex, and that increased prefrontal activity would correspond with decreased activity elsewhere. But we didn't see that at all. In fact, there wasn't a single region of the brain that increased in activity during hand-holding. Not one.

Questioning the Down Regulation Model

I expected to find the traditional emotion-regulation model in psychology, which is called the down-regulation model. Let's say that we have a perceived threat, and that the threat causes four things to happen in the brain. Let's call them A, B, C, and D. They are threat responses in the brain, and they all happen automatically. This is simply what the brain does under threat. If we were to start regulating that threat response, we might add, let's say, hand-holding from a stranger. According to this model, this stranger hand-holding will activate at least one regulatory circuit that will inhibit, let's say, threat response B. If we add hand-holding from a spouse, which we know is more effective, this might activate additional regulatory circuits, inhibiting threat responses B *and* C. Notice that it is additional regulatory activity in the brain that is causing these inhibitory effects. It is analogous to stepping on the gas and the brakes at the same time while driving a car. If this model is right, then the brain would be most active when you're getting lots of good regulation from a close partner. But as I've said, we didn't find that at all. We didn't find any increased activation of the prefrontal cortex with hand-holding. Everything was a decrease. It was like magic. We couldn't find the *mechanism* of the regulation effects we were observing, and in science that's very frightening.

Incidentally, we are not the only people who have been confronted with this. There's another group that I've since started to get to know at UCLA in Los Angeles. Naomi Eisenberger and her group have also been trying to find the down regulating mechanism of social support, and in one study all they found was a decrease in activity throughout the threatened brain when people had a high degree of social support.[4] It seems like magic is happening, and, again, scientists tend not to like that.

We had the idea that maybe we scientists are suffering from a kind of figure/ground problem, where depending on your perspective, you can see either a vase in the center of a frame or two faces in profile.[5] In traditional psychology, we see the individual—the single person—as our unit of analysis. But what if that's not the case? What if we're looking for a mediating mechanism of social support simply because we assume that it has to be there? What if the regulatory effect is not that someone is switching on an inhibitory circuit in my brain, which is then down regulating my emotions and my threat response, but rather that when I'm with my partner, I'm simply returning to my normal baseline state. In other words, what if I'm not stepping on the gas and the brake at the same time

4. See Eisenberger et al., "Neural Pathways Link Social Support to Attenuated Neuroendocrine Stress Responses."

5. See Rubin, "Figure and Ground."

so much as simply not stepping on the gas? What if the unusual thing, the unexpected thing, the *weird* thing, is to be facing the threat alone? We think this is what's going on.

From this perspective, when we are in a high-quality relationship, and our partner is present when we are confronted with a threat, it is not that our partner's presence provides us with inhibitory influences that are mediated through some additional circuit in our brain—it's that our brain judges that there's not much reason to get all excited. It figures it doesn't have to respond as much, because it's in a relatively safe place. So it isn't that threat circuits B, C, and D are being down regulated. Instead, it's that threat circuit A is the only one thought to be necessary. If we go further away from the baseline of being with our loved one and feeling safe—perhaps we're with our partner but maybe we had a fight that morning, and things are not going so well—we might hedge our bets and activate circuit B as well. If we are with a total stranger, whose behavior we cannot reliably predict, we might have to activate an additional circuit C to respond to the threat cue. And if we are alone (and this is key), we must solve all our problems ourselves.

Social Baseline Theory

What I want to argue—with what we in the literature are calling *social baseline theory*—is that we are not designed, as a species, to solve problems by ourselves. Instead, we are designed as a species to be interdependent, always and constantly to be placed in a social frame, and when we are far from that social frame we perceive correctly that we have more problems to deal with than we otherwise would. This means that we have to devote more energy to solving those problems by recruiting more of our brain's resources. The brain thinks this is bad.[6]

As we know, the quality of a relationship can have a big impact on your day-to-day feelings, but I want to give you some data here. There are two structures in the brain that showed a very interesting effect with regard to the quality of a person's relationship.

The first is the right anterior insula. This is a structure of the brain likely to be involved in your subjective experience of pain. So if this region is more active when the shock occurs, then you will probably feel it more intensely. If it is less active, then you will probably not feel it as much. That is part of what this region of the brain does: it directs your

6. See the discussion on bioenergetics below.

attention to feelings in your body. We found that there is no association between the quality of your relationship and how active this region of the brain is under threat if you are alone or with a stranger. But if your hand is being held by your partner, this region of the brain is less active when you are confronted with a threat—even dramatically so. What does that mean? It means that we now have some suggestive evidence that holding hands with your partner can have analgesic effects—effects similar to analgesic drugs (so-called painkillers).

Here is something that is even more interesting. We saw the exact same pattern of associations between threat-related neural activity and relationship quality in the hypothalamus. The hypothalamus is responsible for, among other things, releasing hormones into your bloodstream that impair your immune system, making it harder for you to fight off infection and heal your wounds. Holding your partner's hand can dampen hypothalamic activation under threat, if you are in a high-quality relationship.

These Findings Generalize Well

This was a very exciting study, but we were left with the question of whether these findings generalize. This first sample was primarily white, upper class, highly educated, and easy to bring in to the laboratory. What about other demographics and other kinds of relationships? One of our first studies was on same-sex couples because we wanted to know whether the results were about relationships or rather about certain types of relationships.

For same-sex couples, we see the same pattern with slight variation. We found that context did not seem to matter as much with better relationship quality. If the primary relationship was good, the couples were slightly less reactive to the threat cue whether they were alone, holding their partner's hand, or holding a stranger's hand. Interestingly, the impact of the primary relationship for these couples was more pervasive, and this may be due to a greater dependence on the quality of the primary relationships. Also, lesbian couples did not show much of an association between relationship quality and brain activity in the right fusiform, which manages avoidance behavior in response to the threat cue, and may also modulate amygdala activity. Gay male couples, however, looked just like our heterosexual sample, which surprised us. It has been suggested to us that men are less predictable as caregivers and support providers, and that the association between relationship quality and brain activity in the right fusiform might be a simple effect of being in a relationship with a man. So, if you are in a relationship with a man, you may need more indicators that the man is going to be there for you than if you're in a relationship with a woman, because a woman will be there for you when you're struggling over something. We do not know that it is the case, and it may be an overgeneralization, but this is what's been suggested to us.[7]

A current problem with much of psychology is that it is largely based on the study of undergraduates. They are easy to get into the lab, which is good, but they are also just about the least representative group you can find anywhere. So I feel passionately about moving beyond working with undergraduates in my psychological experiments. I want to study how people who are facing real-life stress utilize their social networks, and how that is manifested in the brain. Currently, we are engaged in a very large study working with economically depressed minority families and friends.

And we are also interested in better understanding how different kinds of relationships function. So people have recently come into the lab with a close friend, not with a romantic partner. To get a sense of the quality of the friendship, we do not use the same measures that we use with our romantic couples. Instead, we use the Inclusion of the Other in the Self Scale, the IOS from Art Aron at the State University of New York at Stony Brook.[8] It is a simple self-report measure that indicates how much you feel like you overlap with the person with whom you have come into the lab.

We are running the same hand-holding study, and the findings are, I think, very interesting. Recall that when we were looking at romantic partners, there was a strong negative correlation between closeness of the relationship and neural activation under threat. In other words, the better the quality of the relationship, the less active the brain is. We don't see that in our low-socioeconomic-status friendships at all. There is simply no association, not even with the stranger condition. But with the alone condition there is a big change in neural activity. It is the mirror image of the high-socioeconomic-status married couples. With the high-socioeconomic-status married couples, there was no effect at all during the alone condition. So here, it's not that they're less active when their friend is with them; it's that they're very much more active if their friend

7. Please note that since I gave this talk, we have reanalyzed these data, with some differences in the nature of our results. These new findings will be presented in Coan et al., forthcoming.

8. See Aron et al., "Inclusion of Other in the Self Scale and the Structure of Interpersonal Closeness."

is *not* with them, which means that those situations are simple opposites. On the one hand, you have the wonderfulness of having your friend with you, helping you out. On the other hand, you have the terribleness of being without the friend.

The results appear to suggest that under economic stress, the greatest imperative is to never be alone. How you benefit from your social system is another question, but the first imperative is to be with your social system. We actually see this same pattern throughout the brain. These results are very interesting to us, and they have taught us something about the way social resources interact with other kinds of resources to keep us feeling safe and secure.

Bioenergetics

To understand better what I believe is going on with these findings, I need to introduce you to two concepts: economy of action and perception-action links. Economy of action is a principle of any biological system, and it goes like this: If you are going to be a biological system and alive, then you have to bring in more resources than you give out. To give out more resources than you bring in is to be dead, and you don't want that. Economy of action means that animals will, whenever they can, try to conserve energy.

Take cheetahs and gazelles. Cheetahs are the fastest land animals on earth, but they can only run for a short period of time before they are completely spent and have to rest. It turns out that cheetahs and gazelles coevolved as a predator–prey system, and (in a manner of speaking) gazelles know (more or less) how long a cheetah can run at top speed. So the gazelle will stop running when the cheetah stops running. *This is often true even when the cheetah is still right there.* You're a gazelle now, and there's the cheetah that was just trying to kill and eat you, but now you have an opportunity to rest and conserve resources too, and chances are you will take it.[9] This is an example of economy of action. You see this over and over again in the animal kingdom, and our human brains work the same way.

Perception-action links shape how we decide to engage in a given activity and when we can conserve our resources in our brain and in our

9. Occasionally, when the gazelle is significantly less exhausted than the cheetah after a failed chase, the gazelle will actually turn and try to gore the cheetah to death: not a conservation strategy, perhaps—unless you count the fact that a dead cheetah will not pick up the chase at a future opportunity.

body. Our brain plays perceptual tricks on us to shape our behavior. Many of you may know about the visual tricks our brain plays on us. Certain kinds of objects look like they're spinning even when they're stationary, and two lines of equal length can look like they're different lengths depending on how you manipulate the ends. Our brain causes us to see things that aren't really there all the time, and the reason it doesn't as often tell you how things *really* are is because if it did, you wouldn't be as efficient a regulator of your body's metabolic resources. In a sense, your brain is tricking you into making effective decisions.

Dennis Proffitt, a friend and colleague of mine at the University of Virginia, has done research where he has people stand at the foot of a hill and estimate, under two conditions, how steep the pitch of the hill is: the first is the condition of unencumbered standing, and the second condition is the condition of wearing a heavy backpack.[10] What do you think happens? When subjects have the heavy backpack on, they see the hill as steeper. They're not using metaphor or engaging in poetry. They are actually seeing the hill as steeper.

I want to argue that when we are alone, the hill *is* steeper. That's because we are designed to be with other people. The reason that I expected to find a down-regulating circuit running through the prefrontal cortex is that I was still stuck thinking that the human brain should be alone, that the baseline human brain is just a brain by itself. But that's not true at all. It's not that we were *adding* stimuli when we have someone come in and hold the hand; it's that *we're taking stimuli away*, because it is being alone that's adding something. To be alone is to add a heavy backpack, to add a burden. It's more taxing on our personal resources. In case you think this is all hypothetical, it isn't. My colleague Simone Schnall actually had people stand next to their friends while wearing a heavy backpack and estimating hill pitch, and she found that if you're standing next to your friend, you see the hill as less steep.[11] That's pretty interesting already, but it gets considerably more exciting because we can also look at the correlation between the duration of the relationship (how long you have been friends) and the estimated pitch of the hill. And when we do, we see a very powerful negative relationship: the longer you've been friends with the person standing next to you, the less steep the hill.

10. See Proffitt, "Embodied Perception and the Economy of Action."
11. See Schnall et al., "Social Support and the Perception of Geographical Slant."

It's because your brain is making a prediction. If I have to walk up that hill, how good a reason do I have to have? If I have low resources, I'm alone, or wearing a heavy backpack, I need to have a good reason to walk up the hill because standing here I have the opportunity to conserve resources, and that's always a good idea, as we learned from the gazelles. If my friend is with me, then I don't have to have as much of a reason to avoid the hill because my friend will help me if things go bad, or if I get really tired. Therefore I don't have to see the hill as so steep. The hill is more inviting; it is more welcoming. I think you can think of the whole world as a kind of hill, and we're all standing at the base of this world-hill, and that world-hill is a little less steep, a little more welcoming, when you're with your friends and loved ones, because they extend your perceived resources, and your brain finds that it doesn't have to work so hard. Our brains are fundamentally energy conserving, just like gazelles. If there is an opportunity not to do something, then we're going to not do it (speaking for myself at least).

I Am You, and You Are Me

As part of the new work that we're doing, we've added a couple of threat conditions. We've repeated over and over again this same experiment that I've been describing to you, but now we're sometimes directing the threat at the person who's in the scanner, and other times directing the threat at the person who's outside the scanner holding their hand.[12] So now not only are we asking how threat responsive your brain is when the threat is directed at you, but how threat responsive your brain is when the threat is directed at someone else, and we can manipulate whether that person is your friend or a stranger.

So far, we've found that in the orbital frontal cortex, which is involved in evaluating the goodness or badness of things, there is a strong correlation between threats directed at the self, and threats directed at another person. In other words, if your brain is saying, "That's bad," when a threat is directed at you, it's also likely to say, "That's bad," when a threat is directed at someone else. There was more though. The right dorsal lateral prefrontal cortex, which is what you use to regulate your emotions, also showed a correlation between threats directed at the self and threats directed at another person. Only this time, the correlation only appeared if the other person

12. See Beckes et al., "Familiarity Promotes the Blurring of Self and Other in the Neural Representation of Threat."

was a close friend. There was no association whatsoever with the stranger. So you're not having to tell yourself it's only a movie when someone else is in danger if you don't really know that person. That's interesting, too, but it gets even more interesting.

Recall that the more active the insula is, the more you might feel the shock. That is because the insula is part of a network that diagrams your body. The insula, in cooperation with certain other regions of the brain, creates a model of the state of your body. It references you: what's going on in your heart, your feelings, your leg, on your ankle where you might receive the shock, and so on. In any case, in the left insula we saw a correlation of .9, which is very dramatic, between threats directed at the self and threats directed at a close friend. By contrast, the correlation of activity drops below significance to essentially nothing between threats directed at the self and threats directed at a stranger. This pattern generalizes to a large number of other threat-responsive regions of the brain.

From the perspective of activity in specific neural circuits, it looks to us as if the brain stops drawing as great a distinction between ourselves and another person when that person becomes familiar. When another person becomes a part of our social system, they become part of *us*. And they are likely doing the same thing in return. So we become them, and they become us. We extend our self to include them in it. When we become close to someone, our sense of self expands, it grows to include and incorporate other people. We see this in the example of the threat, but we also think this explains part of what's going on with the soothing hand-holding. If you are part of me, and I am under threat but you are not, then part of me is also not under threat. Likewise, if you are part of me, and I am part of you, and I'm not under threat but you are, then part of me is under threat.

Evolutionary biologists fret, and have fretted since Darwin, about human altruism. They get upset about this because it's not supposed to be there. You can explain it fairly well in other nonhuman animals because they mainly engage in altruistic behavior that is either explicitly reciprocal or directed toward genetic kin. But humans engage in altruistic behavior in all kinds of contexts, all the time. With the research we and others are starting to do on the extended self, I think we may be making real progress toward solving this human altruism problem. What if we have been looking at it wrong? We keep asking, "Why doesn't that individual behave selfishly?" Well, maybe it's that the self is not what we thought it was. Perhaps the self is greatly expanded beyond what is between our ears. What we are seeing suggests that the self happens somewhere else, in some space between us and our social community. We think this is a very profound insight into how the human brain is designed to work.

Reexamining the Self and Some Thoughts on Spirituality

Let's review before concluding with some thoughts on spirituality. Humans are the cheetahs of self-regulation. We can regulate our inner world very well, but we can only do it for short bursts of time because the prefrontal cortex is very expensive to operate. If we can decrease its use, that's always a good thing, but it is available to us when we need it. Because self-regulation is costly, we typically see increased feelings of exhaustion and decreased self-regulatory capabilities if we have to do it for an extended period of time. You can only tell yourself, "It's only a movie" for so long before you become freaked out.

Social proximity exerts its effects by allowing our brains the opportunity to conserve resources. We are born to be in a social context all the time, and being in that social context alters our perception of the world—the steepness of the hill of life, you might say. Being in a social context, then, has all kinds of benefits for our health and well-being.

We achieve this, in part, by extending our brain's representation of the self. To demarcate the self very precisely, and to think that the self exists in our brain between our ears, is an inadequate understanding of what the self is. The human brain is designed to represent the self as inclusive of the people that we know and love and who exist in our social networks. They are part of our self, which means that the baseline-regulation strategy for the human is social in nature. Our brains are born expecting our social networks to be there. We meet people in our lives expecting social relationships to form. The strange thing is when we are alone and perceive ourselves to be low in social-support resources, which is unfortunately the standard experimental context for most psychology.

When I first did the original hand-holding study, we got some press, which is every scientist's dream: somebody's paying attention to me! It showed up in the *New York Times*, and for the first and possibly only time in my career I received fan mail. Aside from the fact that I was getting it at all, there was something really striking about this fan mail. It was typically from women telling a story of their husbands getting sick. This is an excerpt from an actual e-mail that I received from a woman coping with her husband's cancer. She said, "He never holds my hand, it's not like him. But after this surgery and all the time in the hospital, he constantly wants me to hold his hand. He reaches for me all the time."[13]

I love this quote because it illustrates so many things. You may not know how much of a regulatory force your social world is having upon you right now because you may be very comfortable. You may have enough money, you may have enough to eat, and you may be in very good health. What we are learning, however, is that a regulatory system is building up between you and your social network all the time. Myron Hofer, the attachment researcher, has referred to this process as a hidden regulation system. It's hidden because we do not always see it until we need it.[14] But it is there, and it deserves to be cultivated even when it is not necessary. It's like having a savings account, you might say.

This is part of the reason why we stress our subjects out when they come into the laboratory. We are learning about how the brain is designed, and what our social relationships mean for us, because we are able to create a situation where the regulation system becomes manifest. When we are not facing a threat, the system is hidden. It may be hidden in your own life, but it is there, and your brain actually *assumes* it to be there. When you have information that suggests it might not be there, you see the hill of life as steeper. This gets me to the very last thing I want to say.

When I was asked to come here to talk at this conference, it was a very exciting opportunity for me. It was also somewhat daunting in a specific way because of this strange thing called spirituality, which I have never been asked before to speak about in any fashion at any conference. I have been asked to describe my data analysis, my samples, and I have even been confronted on points of evolutionary theory. But no one has ever asked me what the implications might be for a sense of spirituality or God. So I'm in uncharted territory here.

13. E-mail to author on February 7, 2006.

14. See Hofer, "Hidden Regulators in Attachment, Separation, and Loss."

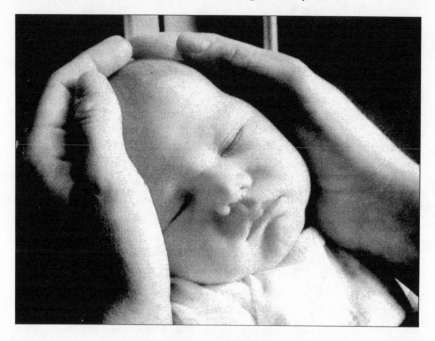

This is a picture of my daughter, taken the day after she was born. Her name is Lulu. She was born on the 22nd of March[15] at one o' clock in the afternoon, and those hands around her head are the hands of my wife. When I think of the data that I have shared today—what we are learning about the brain, and the implications for evolutionary theory—it all collapses into this singular experience that I am having, that many of you have had or will have, of this image, and images like it that I know. This little life, this little person, embodies much of what I want to talk to you about. Because this little person *assumes* those hands will be there. And if those hands were not there, then that little person would not be experiencing life as it was meant to be lived by a human.

Being *held* like that is life as it was meant to be lived by a human. It's part and parcel of what it is to be a person, and it was so from the very beginning of each of our lives. This is not just a matter of the baby's perception of being safe and warm. At this point in her life, it is mostly just stimulation, but the process—the formation of hidden regulation, and of the expanded self—is happening. Here she is. And she's also my wife. And she's me. That baby is now part of the neural representation my brain uses to understand myself, as is my wife. And it's all reciprocated, whether we see it happening in our ordinary daily lives or not.

15. 2011—eleven sleepless days before this talk was given.

I know that Lulu will have an underdeveloped prefrontal cortex for many years. Many of you who are parents know this already, which is why you have spent part of your life lying on your back staring up at the ceiling exhausted. Because she does not have a fully developed prefrontal cortex, she will depend on my prefrontal cortex for some time. She will not be able to tell herself, "It's only a movie" right away, but I will be able to tell her, "It's only a movie" if she finds a situation frightening. By this process, she will contract out, if you will, her emotion-regulation needs to me, as I will do from time to time to my wife, as my wife will do from time to time to me, and so on.

The self—mine, Lulu's, my wife's—has to be reexamined here because it is not clear where exactly it resides in our emerging family. There is some other self that has to be considered, and scientists have not yet paid sufficient attention to it. Or maybe some have, and I'm just not reading enough, but either way, it is new to me. So where *is* this self? If we look for the answer in the brain, we will find that our neural representation of self overlaps with the way we represent familiar others. We will find an extended or distributed self. A self that is distributed across brains, sharing processing effort, not just about who washes the dishes and does the laundry but about who literally computes the thought "it's only a movie."

These processes can seem intuitively obvious when we are talking about children and emerging families, but we are learning that precisely the same kinds of processes occur among adults interacting with each other. Part of the reason that even holding a stranger's hand works, is that the human brain is like a catcher's mitt waiting for a baseball: waiting for social contact and social connection. We are always prepared to make contact, and we will do it very rapidly. Having fully developed brains, adults still benefit from their social networks, and we make use of them to ensure, as much as possible, that the hill of life is not as steep as it could be.

This gets me to the most difficult part. What are we talking about when we talk about God? I don't really know. I'm accustomed to designing research projects with operational definitions and things that I can measure directly. If I do not have those working conditions, then I generally consider it to be outside my purview. But it seems to me that we are talking about a general human capacity for connection, self-expansion, and interdependence.[16] Perhaps we can add another level and say that when we are talking about feelings of spirituality, we are talking about a neural phenomenon that extends the self even further. Extended, perhaps, to where

16. Cf. Thomson, *Why We Believe in God(s)*.

the self becomes part of something that, in a kind of ecstatic and rapturous way, makes the question of where the self resides even more fuzzy.

What it really comes down to is a sense that we are not alone. How do we achieve a greater sense of spirituality, a greater connection to what many of us may call God? I think the answer is to make *contact*, to reach out to social networks, to let go of ourselves, and open up to the possibility of being included in, being next to, being a part of something much larger, which is quite profound. So it is not really that my self is diminishing, but that I'm less and less alone as my self *expands* to include my social resources, some of which may be unseen.

Christian's Response

What I like about the argument is that social-baseline theory seems intuitively true and simple but at the same time also incredibly profound and world changing. That is, what attracts me to attachment theory is also what attracts me to social-baseline theory. I believe that we are dealing here with an honest-to-goodness paradigm shift. Because of training in a particular paradigm, everyone saw one thing, but you started seeing something else. And, by golly, I think you're right. It makes sense to me that the baseline is not the isolated, passive individual, but the socially connected and interactive human being. As a parent of three little boys, I can honestly say that emotion regulation is absolutely at the top of my list, and I frequently tell myself that it's just a movie.

I remember coming home from teaching one day only to discover that Oliver, my youngest who is now four, had found my laptop and had systematically picked off all the keys on the keyboard. I'm sure that the first key was the most difficult, but as Aristotle reminds us, it gets a lot easier with practice. In that moment, my inner needle could go one of two directions: ramp up in anger or disassociate by telling myself that *it's just a movie*. I find both strategies to be incredibly exhausting.

But what you say next is crucial. The more connected we are, the less exhausting it feels to solve the problems of life. The more disconnected and isolated we are, the steeper it is going to look to climb up the hill of life just as if your backpack had suddenly gotten heavier. And what you mean by being connected is the process of extending and distributing our sense of self with others, sharing our internal states with others, and taking on the internal states of those closest to us, the effect of which is that problem solving and emotion regulation becomes a lot less effortful. Said differently, life just got a whole lot easier.

The obvious conclusion to this is that it is good for us to live in community. Life together takes less effort than life separately. And if that is the case, then it is no wonder that life has recently gotten a lot harder, not easier, because we're more and more isolated from each other, more than we have ever been before. It's exhausting. Life in community, by contrast, is far more sustainable, far more bio-energetically green, you might say.

Now, several interesting things follow, I think, from this conclusion. First, it is noteworthy that in the biblical account of creation, it is after the creation of human community—male and female, God created them—that God rests, and in so doing creates peace. It is not good for us to be alone, and in community there is a peaceful rest, which Genesis understands as a gift from God. However, as we know, human community and connection can also be the source of great distress since it is friends and lovers, those who are the closest to us, who can betray us, and not strangers.

If social baseline theory is correct, and I think it is, then what you need are intentional communities that learn to practice restoration and reconciliation, which is to say habits of repair. And, as Aristotle reminds us, it gets easier the more you do it. In other words, you need something like the social experience of navigating life together shared by the early Christian churches before Christianity was enlisted into the service of having to maintain the Roman Empire. Those early Christian communities intentionally worked at overcoming deep ethnic and socioeconomic divides—Jew and Greek, citizen and not-citizen, rich and poor, male and female, and so on—in the simple belief that in Christ those walls have been broken down. It is something like that social experiment that we need now.

5

Integrating Heart and Soul

Attachment and Interdependence

Susan Johnson

Introduction

I USUALLY ADDRESS THERAPISTS ON the subject of *Emotionally Focused Therapy* (EFT),[1] which is an approach to helping people understand their relationships that is on the cutting edge of putting into clinical practice the new science of love and adult bonding. It is a science that has amazing significance for us, for our families, and for how we see ourselves. I will begin with the science of love and give you a feel for what's happening in this field, and then I will conclude with talking about the soul, in particular discussing how our sense of what it means to be human fits into this new science of love. Humankind has always struggled to understand love. Perhaps the heart of what fascinates us is to understand what is most human about us so that we can grow into being more truly human, and at some point I think that has to include the soul.

EFT differs from many other key approaches to working with relationships that have dominated the couples field until very recently. EFT does not teach problem solving, nor does it stretch out long family histories or focus primarily on the creation of insight, and it does not coach skilled interactions to improve communication skills and so reduce conflict. The

1. Johnson, *Creating Connection*. My witty son likes to call it "Extremely Funny Therapy."

ultimate goal of EFT is to help partners *reach for each other* and to *create the attuned synchrony of emotional responsiveness* that builds secure bonds. The reason for this is that evidence suggests that empathy starts with body synchronization and movement coordination: moving together in synchrony creates bonds. Being in sync physically starts to create a sense of deep connection. I have been told that singing together is an important part of the Mennonite tradition. It means that on a very physical level you know about tuning in, coordinating, listening to each other, and creating a greater whole.

The Tango of Love: A Neural Duet

I have found the image of the tango to be useful in illustrating this synchrony. Tango, like a love relationship, is an improvised dance. In Argentinian tango, you don't follow set steps, so there is a sense that you don't know what your partner is going to do next. Each person tunes in to the other and is able to intuit intentions, coordinate moves, and create what physicists call resonance: two elements moving together and tuning in to each other, coordinating and becoming a greater whole. Body language and emotional cues are the music of this dance. Resonance is the sympathetic vibration of two elements, allowing them to act in harmony.

This is a neural duet of matched rhythms, pacing, intuited intentions, and coordinated responses. You see this exact kind of beautiful synchrony in mother-and-infant play where there is secure connection. I want to point out here that the connection is *felt*. It is not an idea in your mind. It is felt through the body, and the resonance is emotional. It is exactly what the attachment theorists say: you need a felt sense of security with another person. If you go up in your head, you lose it. Believe me; I have had many tango lessons where my teacher would say to me "Where are you? You are in your head trying to predict what I'm going to do!" That's what happens to the couples that I see in therapy; they are no longer emotionally present in the dance of the relationship.

Felt emotional responsiveness is a powerful predictor of newlywed satisfaction five years later in relationships. For example, Ted Huston claims that if you want to know where people are going to be in five years, don't look at the number of times they fight, because all couples fight; look instead at how emotionally responsive they are to each other.[2] If they lose each other and

2. Huston et al., "The Connubial Crucible."

mistune, as we all do now and then, their emotional responsiveness allows them to turn back towards each other, to tune in, and (re)create harmony again. To continue the metaphor of Argentinian tango then, dancers can only move in this kind of harmony when they have a felt sense of secure bodied connection such that they can order and shape the signals they are sending and receiving back and forth. With human bonding, emotions are the signals that we send and receive, and they become the music in the dance of love.

Recent Developments in the Science of Love

It is not so many years ago, that setting the goal of creating such a bond in couples therapy would have seemed, in a word, bizarre. Just fifteen years ago, McKay in 1996 made the point that couples therapists had done absolutely everything except focus on how to create nurturance and love.[3] That might seem like a strange thing since that is what most people actually come to couples therapy for, but the founding fathers of couple and family therapy, who shaped this modality, did not have the benefit of working with a systematic idea of what love was. Sophisticated academics are still telling us—I'm thinking here of Marilyn Yalom's otherwise wonderful book on the history of the wife—that love is an intoxicating mixture of sex and sentiment that nobody can understand.[4] They either tell us that or perhaps that love is just frustrated sexual desire. Well if this is true, then we are in big trouble.

Thankfully, the old clichés about love are being challenged, and this is changing our ways of working with couples. Researchers are now suggesting that apart from the element of obsession, romantic love is much more robust and lasting than previously imagined. Arthur Aron, for example, compares what happens in the brains of young intoxicated lovers and of older long-term lovers when they are shown pictures of their loved ones.[5] His conclusion was that in some cases the brains of long-time lovers respond in exactly the same way, with the exact same joy, as do the brains of young lovers who were infatuated. Aaron's conclusion was that if that is true (i.e., that love can last), then mental health professionals and therapists need to set higher expectations for their interventions than simply lessening conflict. But if you are going to set higher expectations, and really shape love relationships, then you have to understand what love is about.

3. Mackay, "Nurturance."
4. Yalom, The History of the Wife.
5. Aron et al., "Falling in Love."

Cracking the Code of Love

Over the last two decades, the development of adult attachment theory and the neuroscience revolution have created, really for the first time in human history, a tested and robust theory of love and adult bonding. Ludwig von Bertalanffy, the father of systems theory, who started the movement of looking at actual relationships in therapy, argued that if you want to make a difference in a relationship, then you have to identify its leading or organizing elements.[6] In the case of a love relationship, the therapist can focus like a laser on these transforming elements. It is now in our grasp, with theoretical understanding, to help lovers create emotional security, joy, and the personal openness and flexibility that comes with a secure bond. The new science of love and bonding integrates a focus on self and system, on the inner ring of lived (emotional) experience, and on the outer ring of circular interaction patterns, which is the dance that people do in a love relationship.

Humans have been preoccupied with understanding romantic love since the world began. I am suggesting to you that we have now cracked the code. It seems to me that all the focus and fuss was worth it. Love is infinitely more fascinating and powerful than institutions of cards, candy stores, and red roses. At the end, I will go on to suggest that we can expand the inner and outer ring of interaction patterns to include spirituality. We can include how the self relates to the existential truth of our basic vulnerability in the cosmos, and we can create communities and societies that celebrate and reflect the best of our human nature.

The new science of love gives us a new view of human nature where aggression and sex are not the main show in town. They are not the most basic instinct; instead, the desire to reach out for connection is. It provides a new sense of how humans grow, develop and change, and for health professionals, at last a clear model for what a healthy human being and a good relationship looks like. It also tells us how relationships can be derailed and the toxic damage that this can cause. As a relationship therapist, it gives us direction and a map to the dance of love and the inner emotional music that defines that dance.

6. Von Bertalanffy, *General Systems Theory*.

Attachment Theory: John Bowlby

So what have we learned about love? What are the core points in this new science of human love and bonding? It is one of the universe's small jokes that the father of the new science of love would be a small uptight aristocratic Englishman. John Bowlby, the father of attachment theory, began to articulate this theory on the basis of his work with children. In its early stages, the theory focused on the bond between mother and child, and it explored the way this relationship creates set ways of working with emotion and engaging with other people that can last a lifetime. Since then, attachment theory has been confirmed and clarified many times over, but it was only applied to adult love relationships in the 1990s. So this new science of love is still very young.

Attachment theory tells us that the most primary need we have is for connection with another. The desire to hold on to another. Primatologist Frans de Waal points out that we are wired to reach out and to connect, to feel with and for others.[7] A picture was recently placed on the Internet by a surgeon who operates on infants in the womb, and he said he used to think of such an infant as "the fetus." One day something happened to him that he said changed his life forever. The infant reached out of the mother's womb and grabbed onto his finger and would not let go. For the first time, he understood that this was a little being, and this little being was reaching for him. John Bowlby would have said, "Of course, this is the most basic instinct of all."

In this theory, emotional isolation is the ultimate enemy of humankind. In adulthood, this isolation is not necessarily an outer, literal reality but rather is about emotional isolation and emotional starvation. A monk who lives alone on a desert island and feels close to his God can flourish, and here we can think of God as an attachment figure. A person who lives with many others, but who feels unimportant to and emotionally disconnected from those others is at risk mentally, emotionally, and physically. Secure attachment is related to every index of mental and physical health you can imagine. If you are insecurely attached, you are much more likely to become clinically depressed, and you are much more likely to have a heart attack or a stroke. Louise Hawkley points out that there is a link between emotional isolation and having a heart attack or stroke at a rather

---

7. De Waal, *The Age of Empathy* and *Our Inner Ape*.

young age.[8] According to her research, you are three times more likely to have a heart attack or stroke if you feel emotionally isolated, not connected to at least one other person on this planet who would come when you call.

Born to Bond . . . and Safety First!

We are born to bond. When we cannot have this bond, we literally suffer. The suffering we experience is a physical reality. It is not imagined, and there is nothing sentimental about it; it is a physical reality. We are mammals who are born helpless, and for an extended period of time, our need for others is absolute. Key parts of our brain are structured during this period of total dependence. It is natural then that our brain codes separation, a felt sense of disconnection, as a danger cue. The primal panic that we feel at moments of emotional disconnection is real. Jaak Panksepp, who has studied brains for thirty years, shows that there is a special pathway for fear in the mammalian brain, which becomes activated when attachment figures are experienced as unresponsive, indifferent, or rejecting.[9] Naomi Eisenberger tells us that the anguish we feel when we are rejected, excluded, or abandoned is encoded in the same part of the brain and in the same way as physical pain.[10] These findings are very interesting and may demonstrate that perhaps a broken heart is more than a metaphor.

The need for bonding and our response to isolation are wired in. This is just part of who we are. Until recently, we have not understood love, so how could we ever grasp or effectively deal with the impact that our loved ones have on us. A good example of this wired-in response is demonstrated in Ed Tronick's *Still Face Experiment* with infants and their mothers.[11] What you notice in these short interactions between the infant and the mother is that all of what I have discussed above happens in a moment of disconnection, a moment when the mother stops responding to the baby. The response on the part of the baby is immediate, patterned, and predictable; and it never changes. The baby protests the mother's emotional shut-down: she turns away, shrieks to get attention, and then she dissolves into emotional pain and chaos.

8. Hawkley and Cacciopo, "Loneliness Matters." See also Cacciopo and Patrick, *Loneliness.*

9. Panksepp, *Affective Neuroscience*; and Panksepp, *The Archaeology of Mind.*

10. Eisenberger et al., "Why Rejection Hurts."

11. Tronick, *The Still Face Experiment.*

As a couples therapist, I see the same responses in my office. We do the same as adults. That's what happens when you are desperate. We often find ourselves caught by this drama, and it is not always easy for us to tune in and to allow ourselves to be touched by the vulnerability, the panic of disconnection. The difference between a happy marriage and an unhappy marriage in the end is not that you fight and miss each other, everyone does that. John Gottman, a primary researcher on marital relationships, argues that the difference between a happy and an unhappy marriage is that people turn toward, reach for each other, and repair.[12] The couples can find a way out of the emotional pain caused by the attachment panic. It is just like what the mother does with her infant.

Attachment theory recognizes the power and primacy of emotion, and it teaches us to notice fear. The most basic rule for human beings is safety first. Safety comes through connection with a valued other. The science of love places fear and how we handle fear front and center in terms of understanding our relationships. At its heart, then, love is a survival code. It is interesting to me—I just read this on the way here—that this also pertains to spirituality. Here is another version of separation distress: "Since I was 50, I've had the most terrible sense of loss and loneliness, this continual longing for him, pain, deep down in my heart. He does not want me. He is not there." Can you imagine who this is? It is Mother Teresa talking about her relationship with God.[13] It's from her diaries and letters to her confessor that were published after she died. To me it is a very moving example of separation distress. You can see the exact same kind of emotional distress here that we feel for our attachment figures in our relationships.

Defining Moments

Let's go back to couple relationships for a minute and look at the most important moments in a marriage: the moments that define and shape a relationship. The first defining moment previously mentioned is when you feel the press of this ancient code of attachment, and you experience this fear. From the point of view of attachment, this is the one perpetual problem in marriage. Gottman says that when you get married, you marry a whole series of perpetual problems. I think he is wrong about that. There is really only one problem, and it is always the same: can you create and re-create

12. Gottman, *What Predicts Divorce?*

13. Mother Teresa, *Mother Teresa: Come Be My Light.*

this lose-and-find-again, this sense of secure connection? The central issue is whether you can discover a viable solution to the relational panic. What we do in the moments when we feel lost, unsure, afraid, and not connected has enormous consequences. Do we reach for each other? Do we turn away? Do we turn against each other?

If you are able to reach out to a loved one, and that loved one responds, then you find a home, a safe haven. You are flooded with calm, contentment, joy, the sense of strength that we call love. This is the second moment. If these moments occur, we can acknowledge our fears and our needs, we can protest any disconnection that stands in the way, and send a clear signal that helps our lover to respond to us as we reconnect. This is called affective dependency. Unfortunately, the whole of our culture has pathologized dependency. We have fallen in love with the image of a self-sufficient human being, which is an illusion from the point of view of this science. We are not built for self-sufficiency. We are built to live and thrive and survive in connection with others, particularly close-bonded figures.

When we are in relationships, even as trained therapists, it is so easy to miss the basic plot of the drama of attachment. It is easy to focus on the surface, on other elements of the relationship, the friendship and the problem solving. We miss the key elements in the drama, which is the emotional significance of what is going on, and we end up not being able to find the love we need. We have to know how to go to the heart of the matter in our own lives and in our professions. The core of the power, the way we work from this new science of love, comes from going to the level of attachment emotions, understanding our fears and our longings, and focusing on being able to talk about those longings in a coherent way that pulls our partner toward us and opens their heart. A safe emotional bond is one with reciprocal emotional openness, where needs are met and responsiveness is accessed, where partners are able to hear and respond to each other. This is the cornerstone of a secure bond. It is from this place, where both people are accessible and responsive, that we can answer the key question in all our love relationships, are you there for me?, with a resounding yes. When this happens, it not only calms our primal anxieties, but it floods us with positive emotions.

Requited love fills us with joy and contentment. We are starting to learn much more about positive psychology suggesting that positive emotion has a broadening and building effect on experience and personal resources. The positive emotions that couples go through are very powerful.

As a therapist, I can tell you after thirty years, they still knock my socks off. Intense positive emotions and attachment responses in key sessions of EFT predict success at the end of couples therapy and show stable results years later. We also see in the *Hold Me Tight* program that these positive emotions can undo old hurts and promote new responses.[14] Secure attachment amplifies positive emotion, expressing itself in play. Daniel Stern argues that this kind of interaction evokes what he calls vitality affects.[15] It creates pleasure and playfulness. It reminds us of how we can engage with the world and how we can feel alive. Feeling alive is one of the great highs of love, and this will connect a little later as I talk about the soul. The word for "soul" comes from vital breath, and so soul is about aliveness and passion.

Neurochemistry, Decoding Messages, and Reading Minds

We now understand much more about the neurochemistry of love. Oxytocin—the cuddle hormone or the molecule of monogamy as it has been called—provides the positiveness of calm and the blissful contentment of feeling that I am right where I want to be. This hormone is found only in mammals, and it is produced in the hypothalamus. If you think about what this little hormone does, it is quite amazing. It deactivates the amygdala, which is your threat detector, it lowers stress hormones, and it turns on the reward centers in the brain. It really is the neurochemical basis of romantic love. We have known for a long time that we are flooded with it at orgasm and when mothers breastfeed a baby. But now it appears that you only need to show people a picture of their loved one, or allow them to be close to the person they love, even just thinking about their loved one triggers a rush of this cuddle hormone.[16]

14. Johnson, *Hold Me Tight*.

15. Stern, *The Present Moment in Psychotherapy and Everyday Life*.

16. I recently got a proposal in the mail for oxytocin-enhanced EFT. A company has apparently figured out how to put oxytocin into a nasal spray (coming soon to a pharmacy near you). I have an image of people going into the pharmacy, putting this nasal spray up their nose, and turning and falling in love with their pharmacist. So how about massive doses of a pill instead of all these tedious marriage-education programs and marital therapy? I don't think it will work. Can't you imagine an interaction of somebody who puts Oxytocin up their nose or takes a pill and says to their partner, "I love you passionately," and their partner says, "That's just the Oxytocin talking"? We know how to create the interactions that turn this body chemistry on and off as part of the process of therapy and as education. I believe that when we get powerful bonding events that we are flooded with the Oxytocin hormone, and that will be our next research project. Having

Oxytocin also improves mind reading, our way of understanding the expression on people's faces, especially if those expressions are subtle or ambiguous. Most messages in love relationships are indeed subtle and ambiguous, and do demand decoding. Try a simple one called "I am too tired for sex tonight." This is loaded, and you can take your pick as to what it might mean. You could translate this as, "I am too tired," but maybe it means "I am tired of you" and possibly "you will never have sex with me again." The mind-reading study by Domes shows that oxytocin promotes deeper processing, more accurate translation of these social cues.[17] It also interacts with dopamine to block habituation receptors in the brain, so that suggests that familiarity does not necessarily kill romantic love or sexual passion, which is a myth that we have put into this box called love because we have not understood it at all.

The Protest Polka

What happens when we cannot find a way to step out of this primal panic, when we cannot keep our balance and reach for our partner in a positive way? We really only have two secondary strategies to deal with this sense of emotional disconnection. When we get distorted or ambiguous signals, we either turn the signals up, or we turn them down. As a baby does through crying in protest, we yell, we scream, we shout, we criticize, and we poke. This is our way of asking, "Where are you?," but unfortunately it is usually in code. As one of my couples said, "So let's get it straight, when she says to me, 'You haven't done any of the chores on the fridge,' what she really means is, 'I'm lonely and sad and I need your attention and for you to come and cuddle me'?" To which she responded "Yes, that's about it," and then she added, "if you were my soulmate, you'd know that's what I meant."[18] So, we up the ante, we turn things up, we get into rage, and we push people to respond. We get more and more wound up, and they do start to respond to us. The trouble is that at this point we are up on the ceiling, flooded with emotion, and that can be very aversive for us and for our partner.

---

said that, someone just found out that chocolate triggers Oxytocin, which is why it is a good idea to give chocolates to your sweetie on Valentine's Day—not jars of pickles.

17. Domes et al., "Oxytocin Improves 'Mind-Reading' in Humans."

18. Now, just to say, that is not really fair. You have to be able to say where you are, and you cannot ask your partner to know that simply by how you are acting.

Alternatively, we shut off. We say things such as "I'm fine by myself. I believe in soothing myself. I can go to Yoga three times a day, I can go do my meditation, I can eat good things for me. I can tell myself good things, and everything will be fine." It is very popular in our culture to say that we are fine by ourselves. Bowlby would call that an avoidant attachment. All it means is that you have not found a way to turn and to connect with other people. If used frequently and habitually, both of these strategies simply drive people away and generate more isolation and alienation. People who use these strategies habitually, for example, show higher blood pressure in the presence of their partners compared to when their partner is absent. There is no safe haven here. They feel more at risk around their partner than when they are alone.

This is perhaps why the most common pattern in distressed relationships is called demand-withdraw. I call it the protest polka. This is a stable dance where each person dips into these anxious-demanding or avoidance-shutdown strategies where they constantly trigger each other's panic and sense of isolation. This is the deep structure underlying distressed partners' interactions. Here we have a map not only to the internal world of what's going on with a couple now, but also to the external world of how they interact and how they dance.

The Dance of Love

I need to make a comment here about relationship stress. Some say that romantic love by nature is short lived, and that this explains why so many of us are distressed in relationships. One theory argues that romantic love is only supposed to last four years or until your youngest child can walk away. Consequently, so they say, marriage is doomed as an institution because we are not meant to be monogamous. I would like to give you an alternative to that theory. Marriage has changed drastically in the last few decades. It is no longer based on economic survival, but for most of us it is based on love and bonding. Only sixty years ago surveys suggest that love was way down the list of criteria for marriage.[19] For most of us, this is no longer the case. Our families are based on a sense of love and bonding. We also need love more and more from our partner because we live in a more isolated and isolating world. If this is true, we really need to understand this love relationship. Some of us have never seen two adults in love and noticed how

19. Coontz, *Marriage, A History.*

they dance together. It is hardly surprising that, not understanding love, we have been massively unsuccessful in our love lives. The good news is that while we may not have learned how to make love work growing up, we are now beginning to understand what the dance of love looks like. We also know that we are naturally social monogamous animals. We do best, and we prefer to live, in the shelter of long-term loving connection. When we lose a partner, most of us turn around and look for another one.

Dependency, Trauma, and Shame

Those of us who work in the field of mental health and therapy have given dependency a bad name. Clients come in ashamed of their need for comfort and care, calling themselves "codependent." You might expect men to feel the shame of that, but women feel it too. Let me be perfectly clear: effective dependency makes us stronger as individuals. In a safe-haven relationship, we define ourselves positively, we become more coherent about who we are, and we can articulate that more clearly and powerfully. Judith Feeney did a beautiful study on young career women and found that young career women who feel securely attached to their partners are more confident out in the world, they are less intimidated, they are more effective, and they reach their career goals sooner.[20] This is very interesting research because it suggests that resilience is a primary factor of our relationships with others.

In facing the perils of the world, and specifically in dealing with trauma, it is generally speaking the case that what happened is not what is important. The results of trauma are not about trauma history. What is important is whether you can seek comfort in the arms of another. If you can do that, then you can face the worst that the world has to offer and you can find a way to survive. Soothing connection with others gives us strength, gives us resilience, and allows us to deal with trauma.

When you help partners shape a loving bond, you strengthen each person's ability to deal with the dangers life throws in the path. It allows healthy connection and acknowledges that relationships help us regulate our emotions. Jack Kornfield in *A Path with Heart* says that in a vibrant and safe relationship, we can let ourselves be carried by the river of feeling.[21] The river of feeling tells us what we need or takes us to the universe, communicates with other people: we can let ourselves be carried by this river of feeling because

20. Feeney, "The Dependency Paradox in Close Relationships."
21. Kornfield, *A Path With Heart.*

we know how to swim. We know how to swim, and part of that is we know that we're not alone being carried by that river. We can turn to other people and can engage with them and get them to help us with that emotion.

A loving relationship is the most powerful antidote to the corrosive effects of shame. We work with stroke survivors in Ottawa. One stroke victim voiced his pain by saying, "I didn't listen to the doctor. That's why I had a stroke. You're better off without me. You should leave." His wife turned to him during a therapy session at our center and said to him, "No. Stroke or no stroke, you are mine. You are my man. You are my precious one. We belong together. We'll deal with this together." And they did. He had a massive stroke when he was forty-three, and by the time he was forty-eight he had gone into training and had become a special kind of carpenter. He had created a whole new life for himself, which he could not have done without her.

Emotional Presence and Forgiveness

When we understand our attachment, we also understand other aspects of relationship such as forgiveness and sex. Forgiveness has been part of religious traditions all down the ages, and it is not an easy thing to do. C. S. Lewis once commented that everybody thinks forgiveness is a good idea until they actually have something to forgive. Just to give you a sense, these couples are forgiving things such as choosing to captain a national team to win a championship instead of being at the hospital when his first baby is born; being so numbed out and terrified that when his wife has a miscarriage, he tells his sister to take her to the hospital and he doesn't have time, he'll be there later. Let's say somebody is having an affair. How do you heal these kinds of violations of human connection? You can apologize a thousand times, saying something like, "I'm sorry, okay. How many times do I have to say I'm sorry?" That does not work.

In our recent research on forgiveness, we have discovered that there is only one kind of apology that works.[22] What we see in our research on forgiveness is that for me to forgive you for not being there when I desperately needed you, I have to be able to speak my pain and I have to look into your face, and I have to see that my pain hurts you. Then you have to tell me that you feel sad and remorse, regret, and that you feel my pain. Then I

22. See Makinen and Johnson, "Resolving Attachment Injuries in Couples Using Emotionally Focused Therapy."

take the risk of asking you for what it was I needed at that moment of pain, and this time you are there, and you respond. I ask you for reassurance and you are there. It is a repairing reenactment of the original injury. We know this works. All the people who were able to do this with one significant injury, healed their relationship at the end of this research project, went into forgiveness, increased their trust, and were still together three years later. This is very hopeful, and the new science of love is helping us to understand elements of relationships that we really have not understood before.

Emotional Presence and Sex

In this culture, we have taken sex out of the context of bonding, and consequently we have misunderstood this central aspect of being human. I am not exaggerating when I say that all the research suggests that the people who have the best sex and who enjoy sex the most are people in long-term, loving relationships. What we see in the literature is that practice *and* emotional presence makes perfect in sexuality. We are learning that the basic ways of dancing relationally happen in the bedroom as well: how we regulate our emotions, how we reach out to our partner, whether we get completely flooded and anxious and try to control everything, or whether we shut everything down and turn away from our partner.

I suggest in *Hold Me Tight* that there are three kinds of sex. First, there is what I call synchrony sex. If you ask these people why they make love, they'll tell you "because it feels good and it's wonderful and they want to be close. I never feel so close to my partner. I feel desired. It's our special moment. It's a very intimate kind of dance. Those are securely attached folks. If you listen to anxiously attached folks, they say, "Well, you know, I like making love, but really I like, I like the affection most. Mostly that's what I want, that's when I know that she loves me. That's the important thing for me. Actually, I like the cuddling after sex more than the sex." What they're really telling you is that their main reason for making love is solace, and that they are not really focused on the erotic part of sexuality. If you talk to people who don't trust other people and who avoid and shut down their emotions in sexuality, they will tell you that the main reason for making love is sensation. Sensation and performance. This is very interesting because in our society this passes for real sexuality, but it isn't because it is cut off from your emotional life. You're denying your need for bonding. So, it's sort of one-dimensional, and if you focus on sensation and performance, you will also need more and more sensation and performance. Yet somehow, we elevate this as fascinating, sexy, and interesting.

Connecting Religion and Science: Conceptions of Soul

Consider now the example of the Dalai Lama. He is a monk, he lives alone, and he spends six hours a day in meditation. You might think that, if anyone is, he is a counterexample to what I have been saying so far. If you listen to him talk, however, he is constantly mentioning his mother. He says that he carries her love inside of him, and that this calms him down and allows him to adopt the nonviolent stance that he believes in. He also teaches his monks to yell, "Mother!" when they are afraid. This may sound strange to you, but it is not strange because we know that you can prime the attachment system by subliminally mentioning the name of the people that you love. When you do so, you calm down, you regulate your emotions, and you are much more open and compassionate to other people.

This example of the Dalai Lama gets me to spirituality, although as you will see there is a sense in which I have been talking about spirituality all along. Attachment theory is a developmental theory and a theory of growth. The securely attached are more able to optimally regulate and explore their emotions, to maintain balance, to be less reactive, to more flexibly process information, to be curious, to tolerate uncertainty and ambiguity. They are more able to process and integrate experience and information into a coherent whole. They are more coherent, positive, articulate about their sense of self and who they are, more trusting and open to others, responsive to others, compassionate, and empathic. In brief, they are more able to be present in the moment with self and others, open, aware, and nonjudgmental. There are about four studies on this.[23] Using different language, we can say that they are more mindful and more soulful.

"Mindfulness" is the English translation of the Pali word *sati*, which means open awareness, focused attention, and acceptance. By the way, in Chinese calligraphy the character for *mindfulness* is composed of two interactive figures, signifying the heart and the mind coming together. It is fascinating to me that we are starting to link the science of love with individual functioning and religious practices of mindfulness. Therapy, practiced as the experiential approach to attachment theory as it is in EFT, is a spiritual practice.

23. Mikulincer and Shaver, *Attachment in Adulthood.*

EFT focuses on growth and having a more awakened heart and mind. It focuses on deepening awareness, on being present to the process of the stream of experience with openness and acceptance. It acknowledges how many emotional coping strategies perpetuate and create suffering. The Persian poet Rumi says somewhere that the cure for the pain is the pain. The idea is that you have to be able to sit with the pain—tolerate it and explore it—in order to cope with it.

We promote conscious reflection, seeing the whole, a metaperspective, making things coherent. We cultivate compassion for the self and other, responsiveness validating the need for refuge. Thich Nhat Hanh recommends that you turn to your partner for refuge and safety, and that you take care just like a parent takes care of a child of the softer, more vulnerable scared parts of yourself. We validate vulnerability and interdependence and our need to depend on others in mindfulness in the spiritual traditions. In your spiritual tradition, Anabaptism, you talk about the need for community and connection. This resonates with attachment theory in psychology. As a developmental theory, the new attachment science tells us the essence of a human being is not aggression, inquisitiveness, or sexuality. The essence of man is his need to connect with others, this heart connection is essential to survival and to growth, to being fully and optimally alive to the soul.

"Soul" is the English translation of the Greek word *psyche,* which means vital breath or living. It is synonymous with *essence,* the essence of us, and with aliveness. Psychology is supposed to be the study of the soul, which is fascinating when you think about it. The goal of a humanistic attachment-oriented therapy is then soul searching: to move deeper into our hearts and minds and to integrate ongoing experience into a coherent whole that is true to the essence of who we are as humans so that we can then be more intensely real, here, alive and connected to our fellows. Karen Armstrong, in her beautiful book *The Case for God,* argues that religion is a practical discipline the goal of which is to live creatively, peacefully, and joyously with a reality that we cannot solve.[24] The importance of belief, of *credo,* is to say that I commit and engage myself in this way of life. The point of religion, then, is to live intensely and richly in the here and now, living lives overflowing with significance.

24. Armstrong, *The Case for God.*

Coming Back to Love: Becoming Human (Again)

Understood in this way, the new science of love and the practices of both religion and therapy resonate in their vision of what it means to be more fully human. For us human beings, who are born to bond, significance is found chiefly in our connection with others. Raymond Carver, in his beautiful poem "Late Fragment," puts it this way when asking what he wanted in life: "To call myself beloved. To feel myself beloved on earth."[25]

This is where love, spirituality, and therapy all come together, it seems to me. This new science of bonding offers us a more positive, new way of seeing human beings and human nature. It offers us a new way of seeing the task of therapy and education and a way forward into a different kind of world, a world where we honor our deep desire to belong. Where we have a felt sense of connection to our own soul, to others, and to our world. A world where we create real human societies based on this innate need for connection. We come back, we always come back—in religion, in mysticism, in romance, and in families—to love. In attachment, love calms and restores balance and equilibrium, promotes growth and exploration, expands and orders inner and outer worlds, allows for a world based on trust, and touches our most human quality that we all share: our vulnerability. In the soul practices of spirituality, it is the same.

There is an old hymn called "Abide with Me."[26] Through all my cynicism and repudiations of doctrines and dogmas, I am still fascinated by the fact that when I hear this hymn sung, it touches something deep inside me—whether you call it my heart or my soul—and it makes me weep. I think it is a hymn about attachment:

> Abide with me; fast falls the eventide.
> The darkness deepens; Lord with me abide.
> When other helpers fail and comforts flee,
> Help of the helpless, O abide with me.

I think that's a prayer for us all.

25. Carver, *A New Path to the Waterfall*, 122.

26. Lyte, *Remains of Henry Francis Lyte*, 119. Henry Francis Lyte wrote "Abide with Me" in 1847 while he was dying from tuberculosis.

76

Christian's Response

I find myself resonating deeply with your part-observation, part-claim that we come back in religion, in mysticism, in romance, and in families to love. In coming back to love, the implication is that we have also gone out from love. That the going out from love and the return to love is the heartbeat of life.

John Bowlby famously said that all of us from the cradle to the grave are happiest when life is organized as a series of excursions, long or short from the secure base provided by our attachment figures. It feels to me as if this conference is an excursion in which we come back to love. Jesus of Nazareth during his excursion on earth taught us to call God *Abba*—a loving Father from whom we go out in exploration discovering all sorts of stuff, and into whose arms we can return. Even as Jesus did on the cross, we come back—like he did—to love.

I resonate with your claim that the essence of what it means to be human is to connect—the claim not only that connection is essential for survival, but also that is essential to being fully alive, to thrive, to be happy. There are many rival accounts of happiness that in one way or another want to suggest to us that wealth or success counts for happiness. But I think most of us have figured out by now that a house is not necessarily a home, and a home is not necessarily a house.

What we have here is an entirely different account of what it means to be human, and I wonder (since I'm a philosopher), I wonder what might have happened if this country's founding document had operated not on social-contract theory, which understands everything essentially as about bargains, but with attachment theory, which understands that human relationships are really about bonds. Can you imagine? What a fun thought! Actually, I can imagine it. I think Jesus named it the kingdom of God.

Finally, I resonate with the metaphors of sound that reverberate in the air: attunement, harmony, call and response, melody—a melody that can incorporate blue notes and red notes, the major and minor keys of lived experience. The fact that we are born to connect is often a tragic and heartbreaking reality. We get stuck, and it's scary and painful to be stuck. So much so that we don't know what to sing anymore.

And here is the only extension that I wish to add to your presentation. You say that attachment theory is a developmental theory, a theory of growth. Yes, and it seems to me that it is *also* a theory of transformation and of change. In attachment theory, we learn to sing a song again that we have for many reasons (most of them tragic and painful) forgotten to sing. In returning to the song of love, the song of the one in whom we abide, we are changed. Abide with me. Help of the helpless, O abide with me.

6

Narratives of Care

The Echo of Community Transformation

JOHN PAUL LEDERACH

Balu's Song

I WOULD LIKE TO TAKE you to Nepal, to a town outside of Kathmandu, to an area named Bhaktapur. For a moment, imagine yourself in a small training center made mostly of cinder blocks and brick. You are inside a room. The windows are not that big, so there is not that much light. We have eaten *dal bat* (lentils and rice) to our satisfaction. The postlunch period is notorious for people falling asleep, so the people gathered are going to sing.

A young man stands up and his voice lifts into the kind of singing that comes from his area of Nepal. It has what feels like quarter and eighth scales. We would say that the notes do not quite harmonize, but somehow they lilt their way up and down. His lyrics are in his native language, Baluji. The melody bounces off the cinder blocks. It is beautiful. Then suddenly he stops and deep in his throat, a sob emerges; it is a deep, guttural sob, as if he has just broken down or is about to cry. Everybody in the room, whether they were listening or not, turns to see what is happening, maybe expecting tears. But he picks up the melody, and on it goes. Then come the sobs again, then the melody, and then deep sobs, now almost a gasping.

Balu is a formerly bonded slave, a Mukta Kamaiya (or just Kamaiya). He is now about twenty-four years old. When he was sixteen, his community was released from slavery. The song captured the first evening they were released. It is the way his community remembers the first night. There was the lilting melody of absolute freedom, and the deep, guttural sobs of no place to go, nowhere to call home. Their group moved along various parts in southern Nepal until they came to the district of Kailali, which is in the far west. They arrived at the edge of a forest that had a river nearby. Overnight they began to construct little shacks. The group gathered that day is a group of people working on conflicts over forestry, land, and water.

When Balu was seventeen years old, his community arrived in this location, and they were seen by the other groups in that area as encroachers. One evening, his group, the Kamaiya, gathered and they said, "These people are about to kick us off this land again. We cannot move again. It has been too much." Out of that group, they decided to send Balu. "Go talk to them. See if you can figure something out." I have an image of this young man making that journey into the camp of his enemies. The solution to the problem of his community's near homelessness was that Balu joined a forest user group, which is the group that protects the forest. He became a member, and in his becoming a member, they somehow found the space to open up territory for the Kamaiya that had come from slavery. Balu had transformed his enemies into friends.

A couple years ago, I started a long-distance correspondence with Judy Atkinson, a wonderful woman from Aboriginal Australia. I had read her extraordinary book *Trauma Trails*, which documents the history of generations-long trauma that her people had experienced.[1] When the British colonizers first arrived, they actually referred to Australia as *terra nullius*, a land of no peoples. For the Aborigines, the so-called *terra nullius* was a story place: land that holds the stories of human survival across many generations. Land shapes people, just as people shape their countries. The aftermath of a silent war lost, never really fought, left a legacy of displacement and banishment. Perhaps it would be more accurate here to say "vanishment"—to be present but unseen. It is the plight of too many of our long-suffering indigenous members of our wider family.

To imagine a journey towards healing, Atkinson turned to an Aboriginal practice: *Dadirri*. *Dadirri* is to sit in circles, to listen, and to share beyond words. (In a very different tradition, St. Benedict would leave this for his monks as their first and primary task—to listen with the ear of the heart.) Their listening journey went back past recent events of a broken family, past periods of abuse, past addictive alcohol, past grandparents and great-grandparents, back to the ancestors, to the place where the very vibrations

1. See Atkinson, *Trauma Trails*.

of hearth and Earth can be felt. In dadirri, people story themselves back into place, groping to locate the coordinates of their immediate settings, of a lost people violated in their lived histories. They grope to feel again, to feel like a person again. How many times have we heard that phrase in settings of violence and violation? I want to feel like a person again.

The subtitle of Atkinson's book, *Recreating Song Lines*, brought into sharp relief the difficulty of this journey. The beauty of the aboriginals, one of their great gifts to the world, is that they believe deeply that location is found by sonic engagement. Literally, over generations, aboriginals sang to locate themselves. They sing at birth in order to know when you are born. They sing as they walk in order to identify the land. They carry that song within them, as a way to have a map of where they are in their world. You may know this already through Bruce Chatwin's wonderful ethnography, *The Songlines.*[2] At one point in that book he asks his friend Arkady, who is a cultural translator, "Do these song lines actually function like a map?" To which Arkady responds, "Music, for us, is a memory bank for finding one's way about the world."[3] Balu's song came to mind. His very sounds vibrated the heights of this freedom, and his sobs the depths of feeling lost. His cries had a familiar ring, not unlike the cries of millions displaced in Colombia or in the lake region of Africa—not unlike the cries of those affected by the flow of violence in Mindanao, the Philippines.

One afternoon I asked Balu if he knew who Jackie Robinson was, because he was always wearing this baseball cap with a picture of Jackie Robinson on it.

He said, "No, no idea. I just went into a store and that hat called to me. I liked it, so I went in and took it up to the counter. It was going to cost five hundred rupees"—about four dollars. "That was my month's wage, so I couldn't buy it. But two months later, my younger brother got a job sweeping in that store. Eight hours a day, he swept the outside and the inside."

At the end of his first month, he received four dollars, and he bought Balu the hat. Balu said, "I will never stop wearing it."

I said, "Well, let me tell you who Jackie Robinson is."

I described this first black baseball player, who lived separately and had to move in ways that nobody can really imagine, but who in spite of all the odds and insults broke one of many of the barriers that hold us apart.

Balu, in his Nepali, said, "Oh, now the hat has no money value."

2. See Chatwin, *The Songlines.*
3. Ibid.

What happens when we experience even this small little piece of another's story? What is it that we may describe as a kind of felt vibration, when you see this face? What is it that penetrates into our own experience, into the things that we may have forgotten we knew? What is it when we have a connection? What happens when we feel something resonating but cannot easily name it? What is this thing where we sense a shared humanity? I would like to propose that it is the invisible but ever-present vibration of love.

Attachment and Conflict Transformation

I am not an expert on attachment theory. My training in conflict transformation, in particular mediation, was informed by family-systems theory, which was how we were taught to understand relational patterns. But as I started reading more attachment theory, I began to see such an interesting range of points of connection. Conflict transformation and attachment theory work deeply from a relational center, understanding people, relationships, and conflict as linked at a deeper level. Conflict transformation focuses less on fixing things than on these deeper patterns of change, power, perceptions, fears, and hopes.

Sue Johnson's description that secure attachment requires accessibility, responsiveness, and engagement could well describe healthy group process, governance, or decision making. Dan Siegel's description of mindfulness as "paying attention to the present moment from a stance that is nonjudgmental and nonreactive that leads to a form of internal tuning in that is the foundation of resilience and flexibility"[4] could have been written in any conflict-transformation book, about the deeper sense of presence needed in context of high anxiety and conflict. But these things were not the ones that tugged and pulled at me the most. Something else called out. Something beyond the conceptual bridges. Something echoed. Something resonated. Something vibrated.

The Singing Bowl

I first visited Nepal about eight years ago. My passport says that I have been there thirty times since. On my first visit, I came across a Tibetan singing bowl, and on every one of the thirty visits I have bought at least one. I guess I am having a love affair with the Tibetan singing bowl, and my dear wife

4. Siegel, *Mindsight*, 84.

might say that it is becoming an obsession. They are scattered around our house, and I have carried back bowls for friends and family across at least three continents. The singing bowl even made its way as the subject of a chapter in the last book that I wrote, with my daughter, Angie.[5] We were interested in sound as a metaphor to talk about healing and reconciliation. In a chapter that I wrote, I compared the Tibetan singing bowl to the peace process in Somaliland, a region of Somalia.

When we looked at sound as metaphor, we noticed something about books written on healing and reconciliation. Almost every author would say two things. The first is that healing and reconciliation are not linear processes. Then they usually take a breath and go on to describe the phases and stages of healing and reconciliation in a fairly linear way. I would call that a paradox. A paradox is not a contradiction; it is about holding two truths that may be apparently contradictory on the surface but that at a deeper level have a connection. I do think that these are connected. When you are in the midst of healing and reconciliation over deep violation, it is up and down, back and forth, over and again, round and round, and nothing, always nothing, makes full sense. If you stand back and look at hundreds and thousands of these, it is possible to discern a pattern or two that you could refer to as stages or steps. Once these get named, the linear metaphors tend to dominate the discussion. So while authors would say that healing is not a linear process, they do not tell us very much about the nonlinear part of it.

We decided to write a whole book in which all we did was play with nonlinear metaphors, to give them room and to explore them. One metaphor was a singing bowl. A metaphor often establishes valued directionality. Going up is good and going down is bad. Going in circles is not going anywhere. Forward is progress; backward is digression. You can take a whole range of these, and you will find a certain directionality. What we were after was something that began to look beyond how to go from point A to point B. What if the purpose of healing was not to get from point A to B? What if other and more important things are happening?

Let me try to explain some of what I like about a singing bowl. I love the image of a container. The bowl holds a space that is marked by an edge, which makes an inner space and an outer space. The sound seems to emerge from the interaction within this inner space, yet it moves out expansively. In fact, it could cover the whole of this room. Much of the terminology that we have heard over the last few days are words such as *safety*, *security*, and

5. See Lederach and Lederach, *When Blood and Bones Cry Out*.

feeling *safe*. That is something we work a lot with around conflict because conflict heightens anxiety and fear. Often in situations where people have been deeply hurt, sometimes for long periods of time, they do not feel safe. How we create the space of safety is an unending challenge in our work, one where we have to create a safe container. I like the image of a container because it carries a different kind of directional metaphor. It feels like the sound is being called from somewhere deep. It is going deep. It is not trying to go from point A to B. It is trying to touch something deeper.

I also love the sound. Singing bowls come in so many varieties. They were bowls that Tibetans would have eaten out of. Quite often, they are made of seven metals and have almost every note on a keyboard. In fact, the people that are really experienced tune the bowls to make sure they are in tune. The sound of the bowl is based principally on vibration. That is where sound comes from: things vibrate. Interestingly, you feel the vibration before you hear it. How much of human experience, especially those things we do not quite know how to call or name, are things we feel? We do not know quite how to say them. But sound, because it is vibration, has unique directionality. Sound penetrates. It actually moves through the skin. It touches you inside, and you feel it in your bones. Sound is a vibration that moves. Sound penetrates and is expansive. From the center of a room, that sound moves simultaneously around the whole room. We have this phrase we sometimes use for good stereo systems called "surround sound." Sound surrounds you. It holds you. There is something deep about sound.

We all share the experience of being held in the womb of our mothers. Our first experience was one of vibration where vibration touched us; it held us. Universally, if you go and listen to people sing lullabies, you will find that while very different in potential forms, lyrics, and a whole range of things, they have a certain tonality to them that is deeply soothing. We feel held by sound.

I think this is why sound transports us. Several of our senses permit us to move fluidly in time frames. If you have ever been to the Middle East, you will have heard the call to prayer. If you hear that call to prayer again, you can feel that you are back in Cairo or Jerusalem almost instantaneously. If, right now I smell a good Indian restaurant *dal bat*, I can feel like I am back in Bhaktapur. If I hear a certain song, I can feel like I am in high school again. Some of these are good and some of these are not so good, but either way we still get transported. Music has this capacity. Sound has this capacity.

What you heard was a form of resonance. Resonance is an interesting phenomenon when physicists explain it. What happens with the circling of the stick, so I am told, is that the vibrations were gathering and when they find their natural frequency the spike of sound grows exponentially. That is referred to as resonance, or a form of it. It is a very interesting question for those of us who work with conflict. What is the natural pace for the spike of sound to grow? What is the pace a community needs? What is the pace that a person who has committed a violation and a person that has been violated may need? How do we find the place where those things, at some point, seek and locate their resonance? I have noted how many times those terms come into our field. "That resonated with me. That touched me. I felt moved." There are so many ways that our sound metaphors bounce into the work that we do.

I like the stick on the edge. It circles the outside edge, this small membrane that touches the inner and the outer worlds, and somehow the stick lives there circling. That is its life, to circle. I like the circling itself. The stick bounces over thousands and thousands of friction points. If you go too slow, very little happens. If you go too fast, very little happens. But if you find the right pace at which those points of friction begin to connect, begin to talk, begin to converse, then suddenly, sound rises again. If you stop circling there is a decrescendo, from *forte* to *piano*, off into nothingness. Buddhists originally would have used this sort of bowl to start mediation. You follow the sound until it disappears and then you go be in an interesting place, as Thich Nhat Hanh would say.

This circling is less about a project. It is not a project mode that we are in when we are circling. I think it is more a soul mode. It is about finding some kind of meaningful conversation. We might say that circling, using this bowl, creates the depth necessary for voice to rise. So often in conflict we find that people are seeking a voice, a sense of voice, a sense of location, and a sense of selfhood. One of the interesting things about circling is that there are two ways to see it. The first is the more common Western notion that if you're trying to produce something, then going in circles does not take you very far. When we use the phrase, "We're just going in circles," we usually mean that nothing is happening, that it is useless and a waste of time. But another way to understand the circle is that it is coming back and over again, that it is repetition, that it is ritual. It is not really about going somewhere; it is about opening something, recuperating something, and touching something again.

I sometimes tease my colleagues at Notre Dame, who get preoccupied at times with evaluations using a logical framework to show results of the work that we are doing. I say, "Let's imagine that we are funding your

Eucharist. If only we were more effective in doing the Eucharist, you would just have to do it once and it would be over. But instead you do it every day, for crying out loud! Is it not effective? Is it not carrying you where you need to be? Haven't you done it enough already?" Why do we Mennonites sing the same songs over and over again? Is once not enough? I wonder why repetition is thought to be bad. Aristotle says that a formation happens through repetition. When we apply it to our work, especially in peacebuilding, we tend to say that going in circles means nothing is happening. But if we understand the repetition instead as opening space, as what is needed to create safety, and what may be needed to encourage the rise of voice, then we suddenly have a different image.

The first time I met Balu was in Kailali. It was actually in his home area. We had come because we had started looking at the question of how conflicts were so emergent in local communities over access to forest, use of water, and the land. We wanted to meet people who were landless and who had nothing. We found Balu. When we came to his village at the edge of the forest, they pulled their beds out of their houses. In that area, beds are made of a four-post frame with ropes—no mattress, just ropes that cut across the frame. At night, they sleep on them, but during the day, they bring them out to sit on. So, they brought out the beds and formed a circle under the trees where we started talking about a recent conflict that they had over a piece of land that they were being asked to leave. As we talked, people started coming. First there were a few that sat on the beds with us, then behind us and around us. After maybe thirty or forty minutes, the number of people gathered went from twenty to fifty to 150 to 250, and suddenly we had a completely encircled area in that big grassy knoll under the trees, a whole community of people listening to this kind of conversation.

It got a little scary. It turned out that some people who were showing up wanted the Kamaiya kicked off, and suddenly we were in the middle of a conversation where nobody knew what was going to happen next. Ever since that moment, I started noticing how often my Tibetan singing bowl was showing up in real life. We funded for a while a thing called People's Forum Theatre. Forum theatre is often used in Nepal as a way to convey social messages. If you had a health message, or if you had a message about HIV/AIDS, or if you had a message about, in our case, the possibility of nonviolent dialogue, as opposed to the use of weapons, the possibility of participating in a constituent assembly, or just the possibility of women being more involved in the life of the community, Theatre Group would take this and develop a small way of addressing it. They would arrive in a community and they would begin their theatre, and people would gather in a circle. They create kind of a forum around it.

A typical theater-group performance would get partway through this, and they would stop at a particular point, and they would pull people in from the audience, and they would say, "What do we do now? This person doesn't want to let us have this piece of land. What do we do?" Then people in the audience start kicking in ideas, and this is how they have used this form of theater to address many social issues.

The Forest-User Group

This is real people, real life, real collectives. The group that Balu had become a member of, the forest user group, *community forestry*, was started fourteen years ago by twelve people—men and women. Their basic idea was that every local community uses wood to cook. Ninety percent of Nepal needs wood to survive. So those of us in the local community should be watching out for our forests, taking care of our forests. So they formed a forest-user group. That is the group that most uses that part of the forest. They had a long time forming this because the women said, "We won't join unless you agree that every local forest-user group is half men and half women."

We looked all over Nepal, and we could not find anybody that made that commitment except this group. Fourteen years ago, they made a commitment that every forest-user group would be local, and every group would have half men and half women. And they said, "We're going to find another way to validate leadership." So every local group will, every three years, rotate leadership. They will do that by the local group electing one man and one woman who will serve as coordinators. That group will meet with another group, and they will elect somebody at the district level, and that group will elect two to a regional level, and what you had was a validation process that had to rise up organically from the community. Fourteen years ago they started with twelve. They now have more than 8.5 million members. Twenty-four million people live in Nepal. It is quite extraordinary.

They had two fantastic skills. They knew how to organize, and they knew how to protest. If there was a problem with the forest, they could shut down the town, they could shut down the road to Kathmandu, they could do all kinds of things. But they never fully evolved the capacity to engage those encroachers (whoever they might be): the others who would come into their community areas for land, forestry, or water. So we began to work on a question. Is it possible for the forest-user groups, the water-user group, the formerly bonded laborers, the landless, to come together and evolve a way that the community itself holds a conversation about survival issues when such issues come up? Balu's community, the Kamaiya, arrived in the forest not because they were land grabbers. It was pure survival.

Those of you who know a bit of my writing know that my other obsession in life is the study of spiderwebs, especially orb webs. They are extraordinary in showing us how to think spatially. They show us how anchor points are located very carefully by the spider (only a few lines that connect), how they circle that space, creating hubs of activity and connection, and how they rebuild that seven or eight times a day. It is never over. They are flexible in the way that they build their strings, with little coils that unleash in the wind and come back. The spiders adapt over and over to the changing environment, and much of that same kind of adaptation informs peacebuilding in violent conflict.

So we started with the idea of a spider group as a way to facilitate mediation without having a single mediator. Very shortly a spider group would be, if you have a Kamaiya formerly bonded laborers, you have some people displaced from the war, you have a local user group, you have the district local office, you have the local VDC development community, you have all these little points within the community, the spider group would pull one or two people from each group to form a small spider. The spider would move around this space, talking to people, engaging them, asking them questions: who they were, what they needed, what this is about, and then focusing, if possible, toward the question, Could we get together to talk?

Balu's Dilemma

We ran into a problem that we came to call Balu's dilemma. Balu was a member of one of the spider groups. He came back to one of our workshops and said, "I've got a problem and it's getting worse. Here is my problem. I am Kamaiya. I am a leader of an ex-slave group, and they want me to represent them. They want me involved in this discussion to make sure we get what we want. They are worried that I'm involved to do things for other people. But I am also a member of FECOFUN, the forest user group, and they want me to be with them, doing this other thing that protects the forest. Now I am caught between two groups, and I am pulled. What do I do?" Is it possible to have a conversation where we do not take sides? If not, which side should I take? We called it Balu's dilemma.

The spider group was starting to work, people were talking, but the members felt torn. The groups were made up of individuals from different interest groups but as small little units, each user group had to be a microcosm of the bigger thing they hoped to create. So we played around with other images. There are a lot of rivers in Nepal that join and start to flow together. There are rivers that come in from different parts of the country, that flow through different kinds of land, that carry different kinds of sediment, and have different ways that they enter. Inspired by this image, we asked the question How do we create alongsideness? How do we create a space where people flow in a common direction, but where each retains individuated identity and group sense? You do not lose who you are, but you add a capacity to provide leadership for the whole, not just for your group. From this question, the spider groups came up with another image, one that was even more provocative. It is their national soup: Kwaati soup. It is a nine-bean soup. Every bean and lentil has a different fermentation process, a different preparation process. When all those nine beans come into the big soup, each bean has its flavor, but the combination of beans creates a flavor bigger than any one.

So these are the images we played with. What did it eventually look like? This may not sound like much to you, but it makes my heart pitter-patter for a variety of reasons. It took about four or five years to get this particular group to sit down together. If I was to point out some things to give you more of a context, I would tell you that this was in the district of Kanchanpur, in the far west of Nepal. This is a conflict that involves landless Kamaiya and forest-user groups. These were some members, like Balu, of our little group, that had worked for years. To create this particular meeting, it took more than a year. A conversation was opened that included one young woman from a very low caste—a caste from which many women her age would typically be sold into prostitution. She, however, became part of the forest-user group and gained a platform and had risen into some leadership. Folks in their twenties opened a conversation in the community in which people were enemies: the forest group that felt encroached, and the landless group that has no place to go. Now they are holding this conversation.

This is the question I have been after for so many years: how do we create meaningful conversation about things that matter? How do we do that when we are in a setting where there has been violence and violation, and where open conflict and division remain? That is our challenge in much of the work that we do.

Feeling Human Again: Healing and Voice in Conversation

When I first got this singing bowl, I started asking people who use them to show me things they did. So every time I would go to a bowl vendor, I would ask for examples of what they did with them. One time I went to a bowl vendor, and he said, "I am a healer."

This could be good, I thought to myself. I said, "What do you heal?"

He said, "All kinds of things. There are a lot of things you can heal with this bowl. This morning, for example, I had a woman who came from Europe and her fingers were frozen in an arthritic condition. She had not moved her fingers in her left hand for more than three years. So I took my bowl, put a bunch of water in it, warmed it up a little bit, put some herbs in there, and then for twenty minutes I had her put her hand in it, up to the wrist. I could keep the sound going by making almost full circle to wherever the wrist was in."

When he started showing me, I looked inside that bowl, and I couldn't believe what I was seeing: Water was hopping and dancing inside the bowl.

He said, "Oh yeah, bowls make fountains. I do that for twenty minutes, and when she pulls her hand out of the water, for the first time in three years, she could uncurl several of her fingers."

Something was jumping out at me, so I started looking more closely. I got a couple bowls, and I have been playing with water. This notion of natural frequency (physicists put it onto a nice graph, x and y and all that stuff) includes two qualities: one is frequency (how fast you're going), and the other is energy. Resonance is energy. What physicists say is, you can go too slow and it stays real flat. If you go real fast at the other end, it stays real flat. But when you catch the right frequency, it has this spike that rises, which is kind of the way that things come together. It produces not a U-curve, in a nice, undulated fashion, but it often is a much more of a spike.

This was the first time that I could see the energy in the bowl. On the inside, it was bubbling. From the outside, I was not able to see that. I could feel it through the vibration to a certain degree, but I couldn't see it. But here, I could suddenly feel and see the energy field. I go back to the conversation in Nepal. In it I could feel and see the energy in the bubbling up of voice. I am thinking, "How interestingly parallel! These conversations produce a certain energy not unlike a singing bowl.

Remember the Takoma Bridge in Seattle, late 1950s? Wind patterns, not a hurricane and not a breeze, but a natural frequency started to come together and this bridge was not prepared to handle the energy that was unleashed by the vibrations emergent in that setting. For me, the water experience was an almost literal insight, not metaphoric. I felt as if I could see and touch this kind of energy and I wondered how we might have that same sort of thing if we were able to visualize it in terms of the way conflict and, in particular, constructive change emergent in conflict might happen.

I have noticed that metaphors around conflict often revert to things related to sound. So for example, the most common thing I hear across 30 years of work, in settings of violent conflict and war is that when you ask people, "What do you think about the peace process? What do you think about national reconciliation?" They will often say, "We don't have a voice in that. It's out there. It's distant. It's other people that are doing it." One of the metaphors of conflict is often voicelessness. It comes from a sense, especially around violence, of feeling numbed. That is a word people often use. I feel numb, I can not feel.

In Northern Ireland, Carol Kane was working after the Omagh bombing and she had the extraordinary job of taking the flowers from the square that had been left after the Omagh bombing and working with people from the community to mix what would become murals of paper from the remains of the flowers. One of the older men who had lost his wife months earlier in the bombing said, "For months, I have not been able to feel. But when I dipped my hands in this mush, I felt again." Powerful.

In situations of conflict, people often feel voiceless. Usually, we immediately translate voice to power. So they do not feel like they have power. I want to suggest, however, that there is something deeper in this word voice than just power. Voice is about touching a deeper part of one's essence. It is about feeling connected to a wider environment. It is about being located again and feeling human again, feeling like a person, very much like the aboriginals. This was a word we heard a lot in northern Uganda. Sister Mary Tarcisia worked with women and child soldiers, helping them recuperate after being kidnapped, made slaves of the commanders, and after participating in fighting. She would say, "Our work is to have them feel like a person again." *Person*. In Latin: *son*, sound. We are living and vibrating beings. In and through sound and the felt connection with each other, we touch the essence of our shared humanity. For all of us, in the poetic words of Sister Mary, our work is to feel like persons again—over and again, we make our way back to humanity.

The second feeling, metaphorically captured in conflict is the exact opposite and that is the sensation of being overwhelmed by noise. The spaces are filled with loud demands, demands for loyalty, demands for one way to see things, demands for what should be done. These are often competing and exclusive demands, lurid discourse, loudly expressed truths. Think about living permanently in a room where on one side of the room you have Fox News and on the other side you have MSNBC. They are loud and they are going at it. You are sitting in the room and your senses are being overwhelmed by noise. Noise is also sound, but it's not resonance. It's not connection. So I began to wonder about these things. What would happen if we understood that social change, constructive social change, actually emulates the way sound functions? It is one of my curiosities. It is one of the things that I started to explore with this crazy bowl.

You can see it in a variety of the things that happen in communities like this one. You can begin to see how it is a space that is safe, that is gathered. When people speak, they speak in a way that is emergent. They touch a sense of their voice. But they also begin to attend to other voices that are there. There are some interesting things that come out of that. If this were the bowl and this was the water and it was bubbling, can you imagine if we were able to visualize the energy flowing in a collective that is trying to converse about the things that matter? We may call that resonance. We may call it a meaningful conversation. Would we be bold enough to call it love?

Elements of Loving Conversation: Proximity, Voice, and Echo

Let me expand a bit more on the metaphor of sound and suggest ways in which it may relate. The first is that sound is based in vibration and as such there is a proxemics, a close but not too close, to conversation. Proximity shows up in attachment literature as well, with a little different nuance, but also with a lot of parallels. I am using the word from anthropology. Anthropology uses the word *proxemics* to study how cultures feel about space between people. How close is appropriate? So if I had a good German or Swiss friend up here, we would stand at a nice, good distance. If I am standing with the minister of education of Tajikistan and he is holding my hand, and we are walking down the street, and we are swinging our clasped hands and talking, and I am thinking, "Wouldn't my classmates love to see this!"

I started wondering whether there were proxemics to reconciliation and peace as well. I was always hearing something along the lines of, "It is too distant. It is too far away. Our voice enters a space that cannot be heard. We hear voices over a TV, but they don't have a way that it is an actual conversation. The voices are too far apart. We started to explore new applications for this term *proxemics*—that maybe healing and reconciliation need a preferential option for the community, which means the container of the conversational space has to be proximate enough that interlocutors actually hear each other. They are within speaking range. The difficulty, of course, is that national reconciliation requires the whole nation to be willing to enter the conversational space. This becomes very intriguing, so what we have found is the more abstract the conversation became, the more distant it feels. There is a certain proxemics needed.

The second metaphor that we noticed was this notion about voice. Voice is about the essence of me, finding a way to touch the essence of you, to be in touch. I started to note that I am always interested in poetry. I noticed how often I closed my e-mails with, "Stay in touch!" It is a wonderful little phrase. Stay in touch. Stay in touch with whom, with what? Stay in touch with yourself. Stay in touch with me. Stay in touch with others. Stay in touch. That is somehow the deeper root where people gravitate to and when that happens, I think that we get a sense of shared humanity. We get a sense that we are people together, safe and seen or visible. It is not like Judy Atkinson wrote of the aboriginals, "present but invisible." We are seen, and we are held safe even in the presence of our enemies.

I noticed over the last weeks, the third phenomenon has jumped up quite a bit. It is around the idea of echo, that meaningful conversations create ripples. They start to ripple out to other levels and relationships. In this singing bowl, it is happening here, but it is rippling way out across there. The word *echo* is an interesting one, so let me digress for just a minute or two. *Echo* comes from Greek, and it was actually from Greek mythology and the nymph Echo. The gods apparently did not like how much this dear woman was talking, so they cursed her. The curse was that she could only repeat what other people said. She could not originate an idea.

I find this curse all the time in conflict. There are little blocks of ingroup people who all say the same things over and over again and have so little space to say something different because it would come under suspicion. But another use of *echo* has emerged. It is more about the social echo, the ripple effect, the wave effect. It actually approximates what we are talking about in sound. An example is Tahrir Square in Egypt. We have been hearing this phrase a lot in the last month and half: the ripple effect, how things are moving across the Middle East. What is interesting, of course, is that some of these are all three of what I am talking about. Proximity. While it was a national people that gravitated to find each other in the square, they found a sense of voice. Something began to emerge, but that emergent quality rippled beyond borders. I think we find some of the very things that help us define what *meaningful* might mean.

If we were to go back to our story of this group in Nepal, their survival is a question here. One or more of these groups may not have access to the land they need, may not have access to the forest. So how did these two young people frame the question that they were bringing to this group to talk about? As they opened up, they said, "We are here today to talk about this. How could we protect the forest and make sure everybody eats and survives?" How interesting! How do we protect the forest and make sure everybody eats and survives?

There is a certain element of meaningfulness that touches on things that really matter. There is a certain meaningfulness when people are able to touch the essence of who they are, and when they are able to do that safely, in a space, even with those they may fear. When that happens, what you found emerging here was that a group is basically saying, "We think we can learn to live by the principle of sharing. We do not know how exactly, but that is our goal. And it includes all of us, not just some."

Out of that, they began to embody this conversation. It becomes a part of their wider community. It is very much about this kind of a space where these kinds of energies are resonating. I think that becomes what I would refer to as the embodied narrative of care. We care for each other. This at its deepest level, I think, is the spirituality of transformation, which is that constructive change that emerges around and out from a quality of safe space, these containers that care for self, community, and creation. If this exists, it may, on occasion, move like Tahrir Square—rapidly. But it is more likely to move like it has in Kailali. It moves by word of mouth, little by little, out and back, out and back, doing it again, over and again. This, I think, begins to create the bridge between attachment theory and conflict transformation. I think that bridge is love. So let me conclude with several thoughts about these two terms: *bridge* and *love*.

Vibrations of Love: Bridges, Portals, and Circles

Love, like the soul, has depth. It is not a surface quality that has immediate clarity. It is ineffable. We cannot physically see love with the naked eye. Yet, as Bowlby demonstrated, we recognize when it is missing. That was the starting point. If we begin to have the perceptive capacity to notice how love holds, touches, and bursts, it is in fact, simultaneously, about holding a safe space, the bubbling and the rippling inside the space, the rise of resonance and expansion out into the world, but one that needs constant nurturing. If not nurtured, it decrescendos. Love embodies the felt vibration of shared humanity.

The bridge to which I refer is not like the Takoma Bridge that spreads out across a river. No, I think it is more like the edge of this bowl, the sort of marking spaces of the inner and the outer worlds, or like an inlet at the sea, salt and fresh water moving seamlessly back and forth. It is more like that kind of a thin membrane. Anthropologists call this place, this edge, liminal. It is a word that comes from Latin, and it means "threshold," to be on the threshold. A threshold is a space between the inner and outer worlds. The quality of dwelling on the threshold is one of great vulnerability, because you are neither fully in nor out. You are in both worlds. You are moving in between. The anthropologists first explored this in reference to ritual. Their view of ritual is that it is not inherently conservative; it is inherently about birthing things. It births things. When you are birthed, it is an act of creativity and an act of vulnerability. You are naked. We all came out butt naked. So birthing is always creativity and vulnerability. *Vulnerability* has a very interesting Latin root: *vulnus,* which means "wound." The root suggests that vulnerability is how we carry our wounds with each other, how we are present for and with the wounds that we have, and as we are present with our wounds, how healing may emerge.

So maybe it is more than a bridge. Maybe it is more like a portal, a pathway between attachment and conflict transformation, in which we can visualize this notion of an inner world bubbling and the waves that connect and come back. I could actually visualize that energy flow when I saw water in the bowl. In that way, it is embodied. It becomes attunement. Those may in fact be the invisible workings of love. Love, I believe, is about finding our way back to humanity, feeling like a whole person in caring relationships.

Our teachings, from this particular community here, point in this direction. So I would like to conclude with one observation. The most complete understanding of this love in the Anabaptist faith tradition, boiled down to this invisible yet felt vibration of care, was to notice the life of Jesus, who lived his own words: "Love your God with all your heart, your soul, and your mind." And, "Love your neighbor as yourself." That is the narrative of care. Where did I learn this first? Sunday school. Singing.

In the song "Deep and Wide," the brilliant author of this song did not write, "Shallow and narrow, only for me and my little group who think the same thing every Sunday." What is this deep and wide? It is the fountain of God's love. In "Jesus Loves the Little Children," the author did not go on to write verse 2, which basically is, "Why do we stop loving people when they become adults?" What is the basic lesson? We are the creation and children of an extraordinary gift. This creation is under the arms of a loving Creator. We are children, loved equally, but we get our, as they say in Ireland, "knickers in a twist." As soon as it comes to the point that we get into adulthood, we forget that we are all children. I think that is the essence. We learned it, in some ways, a long time ago.

Love has this threshold quality. It emanates from the threshold, the edges, that open the imagination of our connectedness, embodies a narrative of care, vibrates the undulations, the waves, that penetrate, touch, yet surround our very experience and it is on this edge that we find the unending circling journey. It is the one that leads ever in and ever out, winds like a path ever on, the path that we follow to find our way back to being fully human in healthy communities. Then we circle and do it again. And again. And again. And again . . .

Christian's Response

I'll start by quoting Sue Johnson: "And so we come back, always come back—in religion, in mysticism, in romance, and in families—to love."[6] Attachment theory is not only a theory of growth but also of transformation. What John Paul has given us today is a good reason to believe that that is actually so. I want to be absolutely clear on this point because the move that John Paul made just now—making contact between attachment theory and conflict-transformation theory—has not been made before, at least not that I'm aware. This is a new contribution. How did John Paul do it? He listened deeply, and we listened with him, to the story of Balu, whose song transformed enemies into friends.

John Paul notes that there are conceptual bridges between attachment theory and conflict-transformation theory, and those are all true. What he didn't mention is that there is a reason why attachment theory and conflict-transformation theory have not made contact until today. A conflict situation does not fit the usual attachment-research dyads. Attachment research

6. See Johnson, "Integrating Heart and Soul," 76 above.

deals with the mother/infant dyad and the partner/partner dyad. But Balu's story is one in which there is a forest-encroacher/forest-user dyad characterized by enmity. That's how the relationship starts out.

And yet the dyads share a remarkably similar feature: a bodied condition of danger shifts in a moment in time to a condition of safety. In other words, relational connections are being forged, and those connections are shifting the emotional landscape, the internal working models, and opening up a world of possibilities. Surprise, surprise! We've seen that thing before. Now this really shouldn't come as a surprise because I will bet that all of us here today have had at least one experience of encountering someone that we perceived as belonging to the category of enemy, only to have that category blown up by the encounter. We know this. And attachment theory gives us a handle on understanding what is going on.

And what is going on, as John Paul says, is an invisible but present vibration of love. The storied song of Balu becomes in effect a singing bowl, a container holding a safe space. It holds us. It surrounds us. We tune in. We resonate. Bonds are made. We know this. We experienced it together yesterday as Ken led us in song. I don't know about you, but I felt like hugging people. I had a hugging instinct that was very strong. Our brains must have been soaking in Oxytocin. This space became one giant singing bowl, which is a miracle because, I don't know about you, but I have been fighting this space the entire time. But in song, the space was changed in a moment in time. We have experienced this. Love is the bubbling and rippling inside the space, the rise of resonance and expansion out into the world. Love embodies the felt vibration of shared humanity. I'm just quoting John Paul here.

Let me quote someone else. Luke the Evangelist tells us that

> On one occasion a lawyer stood up to test Jesus. "Teacher," he asked, "what must I do to inherit eternal life?"
> "What is written in the Law?" he replied. "How do you read it?"
> He answered, "'Love the Lord your God with all your heart and with all your soul and with all your strength and with all your mind'; and, 'Love your neighbor as yourself.'"
> "You have answered correctly," Jesus replied. "Do this and you will live." (Luke 10:25–28)

7

Attaching Attachment Theory
to Anabaptist Theology

NANCEY MURPHY

M Y TASK IN THIS chapter is to attempt to relate attachment theory to the ethics and theology characteristic of the Anabaptist strand of Christianity. To do so, I'll take a detour through philosophy, concentrating particularly on theories of human nature. My thesis is that theories of human nature relate, on the one hand, to theology, and, on the other, to psychological theory and practice. So, first, I'll characterize modern individualism in the West and trace some of the history of its development. I'll also note criticisms coming from both philosophy and current neuroscience. Then I'll make brief connections to both theology and therapeutic practices.

The central goal of the chapter, though, is to reflect on the understandings of human nature developing in attachment theory. I'll point out that this "postindividualist" theory is actually strangely congruent with ancient understandings of human nature found in both the Hebrew Scriptures and the New Testament. And something very like this ancient understanding is finding significant support in current neuroscientific research.

Finally, I turn to Anabaptist theology, also with premodern origins. I'll give a bit of the history and a contemporary characterization of the Anabaptist tradition. I suggest that some of the practices that constitute Anabaptist life are perfectly suited to the new theory of human nature, providing a way of living in the world that will help us live in accordance with this new or recovered sense of the nature of human personhood. Finally, I'll turn to theology and ask, what kind of God, what kind of conception of God, supports the practices that have characterized the Anabaptists?'

Individualism: Origins, Effects, and Critiques

For modern Westerners, individuals are thought to be "self-contained" in two senses: The first is that they are what they are apart from their relationships. The second is the idea that the real self—the soul or mind or ego—is somehow contained within the body. Here is a quotation from contemporary philosopher Mary Midgley that I think nicely sums up the "moral solipsism" of the modern ideal of human nature:

> Crudely—and we have to be crude here to bring the matter out into the open—this view showed the essential self as consisting in reason. That meant an isolated will, guided by an intelligence, arbitrarily connected to a rather unsatisfactory array of feelings, and lodged, by chance, in an equally unsatisfactory human body. Externally, this being stood alone. Each individual's relation to all others was optional, to be arranged at will by contract. It depended on the calculations of the intellect about self-interest and on views of that interest freely chosen by the will. The dignity of the will rests in its ability to assert reason against passive feeling, which is seen as relatively subhuman, emanating from the body.[1]

Individualism is the product of a number of factors, including sociological and political, but I'll focus here on theology and philosophy.

Sources of Individualism

The first sense of "self-containment" as it appeared in early modern philosophy is well represented by the seventeenth-century English philosopher Thomas Hobbes. Hobbes developed a political theory modeled on the atomism in physics of his day. The atoms exist prior to their relations with other atoms, and were thought not to be affected by those relations. By analogy, he imagined that humans could have existed prior to all social relations. Social facts such as moral obligations and property rights came into existence only as a result of the "social contract," which is motivated by the individual drive for self-preservation. Social relations do not affect basic human nature. I call this position "atomist individualism"—the view that we could be complete human beings prior to any social interactions whatsoever. Relationships are optional, and we choose to enter into them only out of self-interest.

1. Midgley, "The Soul's Successors" 56.

While contemporary Westerners are quite aware of individualism in the sense I have just described, they often unconsciously assume that their true selves are somehow *inside* their bodies. For those who are substance dualists, of course, it is common to think of the mind or soul as *in* the body. However, recent philosophers, beginning with Ludwig Wittgenstein in the mid-twentieth century, have made the further point that we think of ourselves as having an inside, and that our true selves are somehow inside that inner space.

It is interesting that the roots of this *modern* individualism go all the way back to the fourth- and fifth-century theologian Augustine. He was clearly the most influential theologian in the West, in both Catholic and mainline Protestant circles. The reflections that are of interest here began with his puzzling over the location of the soul. Since the soul was not a physical object, the question was how to understand its location in physical space. He decided that the soul constituted a space of its own, and this allowed him to create a very peculiar metaphor that has shaped Western thought ever since. The soul is a space in its own right, and I, the *real* I, can enter into this space. In his *Confessions* he says: "I come to the fields and vast palaces of memory, where are the treasuries of innumerable images of all kinds of objects brought in by sense-perception. Hidden there is whatever we think about."[2]

But for Augustine the important reason for entering the chambers of memory is that in these chambers he could find God. So this image of an inner chamber became a central metaphor or image in Western spirituality from Augustine's day on. It has borne beautiful fruit: for instance, in Teresa of Avila's classic, *The Interior Castle.*[3] However, it did not affect philosophical thought until the modern period, when it was brought to the fore by philosopher René Descartes, a good Catholic trained by the Jesuits and therefore shaped by Augustinian spirituality.

Descartes was gripped by Augustine's metaphor of the self as being inside the mind or soul, and described himself as observing the ideas in his mind. Philosophy since then has been occupied with the problem of how this inner observer can ever be confident that the ideas or perceptions inside accurately represent whatever is outside.[4] One extreme form of this

---

2. Augustine, *Confessions*, 185.

3. See Teresa of Avila, *The Interior Castle.*

4. See Cary, *Augustine's Invention of the Inner Self.*

worry is solipsism: how can I know that there are other consciousnesses apart from my own?

While this modern conception of human nature began among philosophers, it became so prevalent in Western culture that it affects even children. Contemporary philosopher Brian Magee describes his own "recognition" of the problem while he was still a schoolchild. He was in chapel when he reflected on the fact that upon closing his eyes all the other boys disappeared–that is, his visual image of them did. "Up to that moment," he says,

> I had always taken it for granted that I was in immediate contact with the people and things outside of me . . . but now, suddenly, I realized that their existence was one thing and my awareness of it something radically other. . . . Even now after all these years, what I cannot put into words is how indescribably appalling I found that moment of insight . . . as if I were for ever cut off from everything that existed—apart from myself—and as if I were trapped for life inside my own head.[5]

Criticisms of Individualism

Most of us these days are not horrified, as Magee was, because of having been brainwashed by modern individualism, but criticisms are now coming from all quarters. My students studying for ministry quickly realize upon reflection that an individualist view of church cannot be satisfactory. Church growth is not simply bringing more living bodies into the sanctuary. It's not like adding more marbles to your bag; it has to involve something much deeper. Some theologians are making very drastic moves in order to find a rationale for anti-individualism. For instance, an understanding of the Trinity, that sounds to my ear very much like tritheism, is being used as an attempt to model community so that we can learn from the behavior of the three divine persons how to treat one another in society. This seems to me to be a bit of an extreme route to take.

Philosophical objections to individualism come in a variety of forms. I already mentioned the effective work of Wittgenstein, simply pointing out the fact that many intractable philosophical problems are the result of misleading mental images or of poorly chosen ways of speaking. The modern preoccupation with the problem of knowledge has been a

5. Magee, *Confessions of a Philosopher*, 21.

three-hundred-year-long struggle to provide a better account than Descartes's of how we can know that our inner representations in fact provide knowledge of the outside world if we are confined behind the "veil of ideas." Even when philosophy rejected the study of ideas as its proper subject matter (the fuzzy notion of ideas would be better off if it were turned over to psychologists!) and focused on language instead, modern skepticism continued in worries about the "veil of language."[6]

Philosophical theologian Fergus Kerr recognizes the ways Augustinian-Cartesian inwardness continues to affect (infect?) theology. He criticizes a number of theologians, such as the late Gordon Kaufman, who trade "on a radically Cartesian conception of the self." Kaufman wrote, "What one directly experiences of the other are, strictly speaking, the external physical sights and sound he makes, not the deciding, acting, purposing center of the self."[7] Here is Kerr's parody: "Kaufman . . . supposed that it was only when the other opened his mouth and spoke that one realized that a person lay hidden within the middle-sized, slightly sweating and gently palpitating object on the other side of the dinner table."[8]

Nicholas Lash, former professor of divinity at Cambridge, notes that a doctrine of God is always correlative to anthropology. He says that the correlations should be mutual, but he believes that in modern Christian theology the relation has only been one way: from Cartesian inwardness to conceptions of God.[9] For example, when the human person is identified with a solitary mind, God tends to be conceived as a *disembodied* mind. Furthermore, if we can only come to know other humans by inference from their bodily behavior, then knowledge of God becomes highly problematic. Just as Descartes believed that all experience takes place inside the mind, modern theologians tended to reduce religious experience to an inner awareness. Thus, all we know for certain is that we have an idea of God *in* our minds. It was easy, then, already in the nineteenth century, for philosophers such as Ludwig Feuerbach to argue that God is nothing but an idea created by humans.

Another problem for modern Christians is that of divine action. It is now widely agreed that it is impossible to begin with a Cartesian account of the human mind and explain how it could have any effect on a material

6. See Rorty, *Philosophy and the Mirror of Nature.*
7. Kerr, *Theology after Wittgenstein,* 21.
8. Ibid., 23.
9. See Lash, *Easter in Ordinary.*

body. Similarly, theologians are still struggling to give an account of how a mind-like God could have any causal interaction with the physical creation. I've argued, along with many others, that the problem of divine action has been one of the major obstacles to the development of a robust Christian theology in the modern period.[10]

If individualism was inspired to such an extent by the science with the greatest cachet in the early modern period—atomist physics—then it's appropriate to ask what current science has to say. I will not go into the ways in which current atomic physics is no longer atomistic. I'll look instead at neuroscience. One of the founders of social neuroscience is Leslie Brothers. In the preface to her book *Friday's Footprint*, she explains the title.[11] The classic story of Robinson Crusoe embodies a normative image of the isolated individual, and this image has been normative for neuroscience as well.

Brothers chronicles research with primates beginning in the middle of the twentieth century that pointed to the conclusion that one could not derive accurate information about social animals' neurobiology when they are kept in isolation. For example, "the brains of monkeys that are experimentally isolated differ in their chemical makeup from those of monkeys housed in groups."[12] These sorts of findings have led Brothers and others to study specifically the neurobiology of social interactions among monkeys.[13]

Of course I need not rehearse in this volume the criticisms of individualism coming from psychologists and psychotherapists. My formal training in psychology ended in 1973. However, I've been privileged to pick up bits and pieces of more recent work from associations with faculty in Fuller's Graduate School of Psychology and from students studying pastoral counseling. My students frequently discussed family-systems theory, claiming that it gave them brilliant insights into their own personalities and behavior. I've used it repeatedly as an example showing why causal reductionism does not always hold true: the behavior of individuals cannot be understood apart from their family relations.

10. Murphy, *Beyond Liberalism and Fundamentalism*.

11. Brothers, *Friday's Footprint*.

12. Kling and Brothers, "The Amygdala and Social Behavior," quoted in Brothers, *Friday's Footprint*, 45. Kling and Brothers, "The Amygdala and Social Behavior," appears in Aggleton, *The Amygdala*, 353–77.

13. I'll report on more recent work involving both apes and humans below.

I now see, based on what I'm learning about attachment theory, that Murray Bowen did not go far enough in his thought; he was still maintaining too much of modern individualism. Because his focus was on the negative effects of emotional ties, and because he saw the goal of therapy as to increase "differentiation" so as to avoid being influenced by others' emotions, thus making decisions on the basis of intellect alone, Bowen did not effectively escape from Mary Midgley's account (quoted above) of the Enlightenment ideal of humans as guided by intelligence rather than emotion, and whose relationships with others are optional.

What Bowen did accomplish, I believe, is a qualification of Hobbesian individualism; in contrast to Hobbes, who viewed individuals as unaffected by social relations, Bowen drew attention to the fact that within families especially, people's emotions are very much affected by others. This is in contrast to the position that I call atomist individualism—the view that like atoms, we are not affected essentially by relations with others.

My clue for where to look for a true alternative to individualism comes from a dissertation by Alexander Blair, titled "Christian Ambivalence toward the Old Testament: An Investigative Tool in Fundamental Theology."[14] My late husband, James McClendon, was one of Blair's mentors. Blair coined the term "generic individualism" to describe modern theories of human nature, and his thesis is that this unquestioned position on the proper relations of individuals to society has had a pernicious effect on the way modern readers have read the Old Testament. To hold a generic view of individuals is to assume that they are all alike, for all practical purposes (ethics, politics, and so forth). It can already be seen in Hobbes's modeling of humans in society on early modern atomist physics: any atom can be substituted for another without changing the relationship. Blair's work on a corporate, complementarian alternative sent me looking for a "post-individualist" understanding of human nature in the Scriptures.

Biblical Concepts of Personhood

My central thesis in this section is that attachment theories are developing an understanding of human nature that is strikingly consistent in many ways with biblical thought.

In a monograph on the Israelite conception of God, Aubrey Johnson explains divine action in terms of the Hebraic conception of personality.

14. See Blair, "Christian Ambivalence toward the Old Testament."

He says that the Hebrew personality was thought to be extended in subtle ways among the community by means of speech and other forms of communication. This extension of personality is so strong within a household that in its entirety it is regarded as a "psychical whole."[15] "Accordingly, in Israelite thought the individual, as a [*nephesh*] or centre of power capable of indefinite extension, is never a mere isolated unit; he lives in constant reaction towards others."[16] The social unit was conceived as a "corporate personality." He uses as an example the account of King David, who appealed for the loyalty of the people of Judah on the ground of kinship, and "bent the heart of all the menfolk of Judah as it were one man."[17]

Johnson's description of the Hebraic understanding of the extended self was presented in order to explain God's action. The Hebrew word *ruach,* translated "spirit," is an extension of God's own personality. Hence God is *genuinely* present in God's messengers (angels), God's word, and God's prophets when they are moved by God's Spirit. "The prophet, in functioning, was held to be more than Yahweh's 'representative'; for the time being he was an active 'Extension' of Yahweh's Personality and, as such, *was* Yahweh 'in Person.'"[18]

A complementary account of human personality is presented by Bruce Malina, a New Testament scholar who uses cultural anthropology to help contemporary Christians better understand biblical texts. He adopts Clifford Geertz's model of a dyadic personality to characterize the non-individualistic self-awareness of the first-century people of the New Testament. A dyadic personality is one who needs another in order to know who he or she is. Dyadic personalities internalize what others say, do, and think about them. They conceive of themselves as always interrelated, as needing others for their psychological existence. Every individual is perceived as embedded in some other. In fact, there are concentric circles of embeddedness: the family, the kinship group, and perhaps larger social bodies. In short, he says, "the primary emphasis in the culture we are considering is on dyadic personality, on the individual as embedded in the group, on behavior as determined by significant others."[19]

15. Johnson, *The One and the Many*, 4.

16. Ibid., 7.

17. Ibid., 4.

18. Ibid.

19. Malina, *The New Testament World*, 59–60.

I believe that parallels between attachment theory and these accounts of biblical thought will be apparent: we have empirical evidence that we cannot think of ourselves as atoms, as potentially normal if not bonded. In fact, we are thoroughly transformed by our relationships with others. We're not bounded by our own skin. We are, as Malina says, "dyadic selves," or pluralistic selves, perhaps. We function only by having integrated into the wiring of our brains representations of ourselves that we receive from significant others and also by forming a sense of ourselves as they see and mirror us back to ourselves.[20]

We are present throughout our communities wherever our voices are heard. Note how this makes sense of Jesus' most central teaching, "Love your neighbor as yourself." I've seen pages of theological ink spilt on what that means, heard many a sermon, and in our contemporary world it tends to sound as though you should love your neighbor as much as you love yourself. But if you have a sense of self as embedded within the other, as the other being a real part of your selfhood, then it makes perfectly good sense. Love those others as yourself because they are yourself; they are a part of your self. Mystery solved!

At this point I turn to parallels between attachment theory and a small sampling of conclusions from neuroscientific research. As attachment theorists insist, the capacity for empathy is crucial for developing secure relationships. Contemporary neuroscience is beginning to shed light on the brain processes that make it possible for humans to "read others' minds." We have neural systems that are specialized for recognizing faces, for interpreting intentions by observing tone of voice, direction of gaze, hand gestures, and other cues.[21] Christian Keysers and his colleagues propose a theory of social cognition based on the concept of shared neural circuits. That is, it has long been known that in humans and some primates, when one watches the behavior of another, the same neural circuitry fires in the observer as in the actor.[22] For example, if I watch someone reach for an object, this activates the same brain process in me that would be involved

20. The point at which Malina's account diverges from attachment theory regards the emotions. He claims, first, that for the sake of preserving his honor, a first-century man would never expose his inner self with its difficulties and weaknesses (ibid., 52). Second, because people were understood in terms of the groups in which they were embedded, their reading of others would appear to us as stereotypes (ibid., 57).

21. See Brothers, *Friday's Footprints*.

22. See specifically Keysers and Gazzola, "Towards a Unifying Neural Theory," and more generally Keysers, *The Empathic Brain*.

if I were reaching for the object myself. Keysers argues that this same principle explains our ability to react to others' sensations and emotions. For example, touching subjects' legs produces activation in the primary and secondary somatosensory cortex. There was similar but lesser activation in the same regions when the subjects viewed other people's legs being touched. Similar sorts of corresponding brain activity have been found in the observation of another person's pain, disgust, and fear.

These abilities not merely enable us to make *inferences* about others' feelings but, to an extent, to actually *feel* their feelings seems to provide powerful support for attachment theorists' rejection of much of the modern individualist understanding of the person. Sue Johnson says that we have fallen in love with the idea of self-sufficiency, but the essence of being human is the need to connect with others.[23] We use the eyes of those we love as mirrors to reflect back to us a sense of ourselves. Daniel Siegel says that we have to change the cultural message that the self ends at the skin.[24] Similarly, James Coan criticizes the definition of the self as "located between our ears."[25] Instead, we need to recognize that our brains are designed to extend ourselves to incorporate others. He claims that his wife and child exist within himself. This remark makes perfect sense in light of the biblical theories of human nature described above.

Anabaptist Theology and Attachment

What has this to do with Anabaptist theology? The mainline Reformation began in 1517 when Luther nailed his theses to the door of Wittenberg Castle. Charles Taylor, who's written a magnificent book, *Sources of the Self*, gives a great deal of either credit or blame, depending on how you read it, to Luther, for instigating modern individualism. Luther says, "Here I stand, I can do no other." But reacting against both Catholicism and the mainline Reformation, the radical Reformation had already begun to be organized in 1525. It's not clear where all of it started or what all of its predecessors were, but at least one very important event in bringing it together was the meeting on the Swiss-German border in the little town of Schleitheim in 1525. Here leaders set out to write the distinctives that separated them from the mainline Reformers.

23. See Johnson, "Integrating Heart and Soul," 67 above.
24. See Siegel, "Mindsight," 19 above.
25. See Coan, "The Social Regulation of Emotion," 53–54 above.

One of these was believer's baptism. In those days, children were baptized, christened, because it made them part of Christendom. It not only made them Christians, but it made them citizens of the state. So to refuse to baptize your infants was to refuse to turn them over to the power of either the emperor or the ruler of your city-state or nation-state. This led to persecution. I don't know if this figure is correct, but I've read that the number of Anabaptists martyred for their faith during the Reformation was greater than all the Christians martyred during the first three centuries of Christianity. They weren't put to death nicely. The women had it easy; they were drowned in mock rebaptisms. Many of the men, however, were tortured horribly before their deaths. Because the Anabaptists were persecuted so fiercely, they very quickly formed a resolution that they themselves should never take up arms. They believed that if the sword was never to be used to force people to convert to Christianity—less so should it be used for any lesser purpose. So they refused to serve in city governments that would require capital punishment. They foreswore violent defence of themselves or their families and, of course, they also refused to go to war. This was seen as treason, and therefore very severe persecution was "justified."[26]

A second feature of the Anabaptist life and practice is community discipline. This is based on Jesus' teaching in Matthew 18, paraphrased as follows:. If your brother sins, go to him [or her] and reason with him. If you can change his mind, then you've won back a sinner. If the person won't listen to you alone, then take two or three. If that still doesn't work, bring it up before the whole church. And if that still doesn't work, then the person will be asked to leave the fellowship—he or she will be shunned. However, it was never intended to be permanent banishment. It was always a sending away with the hope of bringing the person back. In light of attachment theory, we can recognize how severe a punishment this was, especially given the tight-knit small communities that made up the Anabaptist movement in earlier days. One of the things that seems to be important in attachment theory and in many other approaches to interpersonal health is the emphasis on repair after a rupture.

26. Out of curiosity, I've tried to figure out when the killing of human beings for the sake of religion finally ended in the United States. To my knowledge, the last people to die for their faith were conscientious objectors during World War I, many of whom were Anabaptists. They were not sentenced to death, but they were sentenced to prison, and many of them were treated so harshly in prison that they died of their illnesses and injuries. The irony here is that the Anabaptists were most likely the last Americans to die for their religion, killed because they wouldn't kill.

Another practice for the early Anabaptists was frequent communion, but always with the necessity first to reconcile with anyone you're at odds with. You don't break bread together until you've reconciled. Another practice is simple living so that there would be enough material wealth, material goods, to share among the communities.

A practice that I do not think was used among the early Anabaptists but is significant in both my Church of the Brethren and in some Mennonite congregations is that of feet washing. It is possible to take the Eucharist or the Lord's Supper or Communion, and to make it so ritualized that one can forget that it actually started as a communal meal to which everyone was invited: the washed, unwashed, Jew or Gentile. But when you're taking people's socks off and washing their feet, you really can't get past the down-to-earth significance of the action.

Another important practice is communal discernment. This was based on the belief that the Holy Spirit could speak to everyone in the congregation, and so everyone needed to be heard. It involved study of the Scripture, teaching, and prayer, but it especially involved the chance for everyone, especially the so-called least of the brethren, to be heard in the assembly. Only after everyone had been heard would a decision be made, and a decision usually wouldn't be made until there was consensus.

Contemporary Mennonite theologian John Howard Yoder writes about justification—that is, being set right with God—what others would call salvation. In Paul's ministry, reconciling Jews and Gentiles was primary. The new creation is a new race in which the Jewish law no longer distinguishes between Jew and Gentile, and in which gender and economic differences are reconciled as well. Yoder writes:

> But it is *par excellence* with reference to enmity between peoples, the extension of neighbor-love to the enemy, and the renunciation of violence even in the most righteous cause, that this promise of a new creation takes on flesh in the most original, the most authentic, and more frightening and scandalous, and therefore, the most evangelical way. It's the Good News, that my enemy and I are united through no merit or work of our own, in a new humanity that forbids henceforth my ever taking his or her life in my hands.[27]

27. Yoder, *The Politics of Jesus*, 226.

Conclusion

How does all of the foregoing fit together? Psychology presupposes judgments about what is normal and therefore what is normative. Consequently it is either consciously or subconsciously presupposing some assumption that belongs to the field of ethics. I would say that all psychology is ethics laden. We've been living in a society under the shadow of atomic individualism, with the influence by Hobbes and others, speaking to the necessity of violence in order to form a community. All of modern Western ethics has been individualistic, whether social contract, utilitarian, or Kantian. Now I have not developed a full ethic here, but I've suggested that much is already available in the practices of the Anabaptists that provides a suitable ethic for an attached psychology.

However, an ethical system cannot be evaluated apart from a concept of ultimate reality. When ethical systems come into conflict, they are essentially arguing about what is the final goal or purpose of human life. Without some concept of ultimate reality, God, or simply the universe itself, or some other such concept, it is not going to be possible to settle arguments between ethical systems.

The next step in the development from scientific and psychological work, through ethics to theology, would be to develop a concept of God that is consistent with the concept of human nature that I see being developed in attachment theory. Let me recall some of Jesus' teachings. He did not stop with "Love your neighbors." He went on to say, "'You have heard that it was said, "You shall love your neighbor and hate your enemy." But I say to you, Love your enemies and pray for those who persecute you'" (Matt 5:43–44, NRSV). But why should Jesus' disciples take this hard road? Jesus says in John's gospel, "I am in the Father, and the Father is in me" (14:11, NRSV). In light of the concept of selves embedded in other selves, I think we can make more sense of that Johannine passage than perhaps before. Jesus came to conceive of himself as embedded in the person of his Father, God. Jesus is inviting us to become children of the God who is characterized by love, by the kind of love that makes the rain to fall on God's friends and enemies alike. This is what he means by being perfect as his heavenly Father is perfect. So Jesus is inviting us to embed our very selves into the person of Jesus' own Father. If we do, we'll never be alone again. We'll always be attached to another who accepts and affirms us, allowing us to be fully ourselves.

Christian's Response

Coming out of modernity and the legacy of Augustine and Hobbes, we need to think very differently about what it means to be human, what it means to have a sense of self, and the extension of our sense of self beyond our skin. We are having to locate it *not* in the space between our ears, but in the space between friends, lovers, and family members. The old legacy's picture of what it means to be human is quite simply false, and the Bible got this one right.

This has enormous consequences in the area of philosophical ethics, or how we conceive of our moral life. Ethics, from the ancient Greeks to modern folk, has assumed that the basic unit of analysis is the individual or a collective group facing a choice. Virtue theory, utilitarianism, deontological, social contract, and rational choice; it doesn't matter which one you pick. What we are learning is that the basic unit of analysis is in fact the patterned dynamics of you and me. The ethical situation is not an individual facing a choice, it is dyad in the midst of a dance. It is noteworthy that something like that didn't dawn on philosophers until about the 1960s when there were enough female philosophers to get an ethic of care off the ground.

If attachment theory is true, which I believe that it is, then we are in a position to claim that love is not only natural, but it is a way of survival happened upon by the human animal. From this realization, it may be possible to articulate a politics of love. I don't know all the details of what that would look like, but it will include the insight that it is good for us to be connected, and I will bet my bottom dollar that it will look a lot like what Jesus of Nazareth called the kingdom of God as understood by the early Anabaptist movement, and articulated so elegantly and concisely by Nancey.

Bowlby's perspective of a happy life as a series of excursions from and back to a secure attachment, and human beings as born to connect, has consequences not only for our view of what it means to be human but also for our view of the world and our view of God. This is not so surprising because our anthropology, our cosmology, and our theology are tuned in to each other. So instead of humans as essentially selfish, the world as essentially inhospitable, and God as essentially a judge waiting to punish or be appeased, you now have a human being who is essentially born to bond, a world as essentially hospitable, and God as essentially a loving parent waiting for all creation to come home. I don't know what you want to call that, but I will call that gospel. That to me is good news.

It seems to me that we are not on the way to solving the problem of altruism; we are on the way to *dissolving* the problem of altruism. If you look at human beings as essentially selfish, then to give of yourself is going to be puzzling, and you will want to invent a term such as altruism to name that irrational act. But if you start from a perspective of born-to-bond and attunement, resonance, and dyads in the midst of a dance, then when something happens and there is disharmony and conflict (and, yes, selfish and destructive behavior too)—because you've moved from a *we* to a *me or you*, which by the way is enormously costly and exhausting (war being the most costly of them all)—then you will want to return to your most natural state, which is back to the we of resonance and the harmonious song of love.

I'm not trying to be a fairy-tale romantic. We've had plenty of those, and we are not in need of more. I'm simply saying that love moves with the grain of the universe and with the flow of survival and life. I'm not denying that bad things happen; I'm saying that when they do, we will want to return to our most natural state, which, as Jim Coan reminds us, is being held.

With the help of Bowlby, and the insights of attachment theory, we have gone from Darwin to Jesus, and I'm tempted to say that we have done so seamlessly. From this point of view, as Nancey explored so beautifully, the witness of the early Anabaptists makes a whole lot of bioenergetical sense. The moral character of God is revealed in Jesus' vulnerable enemy love and renunciation of dominion. Imitation of Jesus constitutes a social ethic—a new way of peace, which is actually a very old way, of love. The Bible calls it *shalom*.

8

Attachment to Place and Nature in Our Search for Shalom

Janel Curry

T HE CAPACITY TO EXPERIENCE and develop healthy relationships is closely tied to experiences of early positive attachment to others. Without these positive early experiences, individuals cannot easily develop a capacity to relate meaningfully to others. Some psychologists have posited that this same interpersonal dynamic may apply to the relationship between humans and nature.[1] I want to argue, though, that the concept of nature is not rich enough to capture the multifaceted aspects of this relationship. The complexity of these relationships is more akin to Aldo Leopold's land ethic, where he asks us to enlarge the boundaries of our concept of community to include the natural world.[2] In seeing ourselves and acting as a member of this larger community, we express and learn healthy dependency and interdependency with other individuals, the human community, and the natural world.

Personhood and Attachment to Place

What does this vision of personhood attached to the larger community as described by Leopold look like? Recently I took a group of students to New Zealand to study the topic of sustainability. While many people think of sustainability as just environmental, in New Zealand it is framed as an interrelational whole of environmental, social, economic, and cultural

1. Jordan, "Nature and Self—An Ambivalent Attachment?"
2. Leopold, *A Sand County Almanac*, 204.

sustainability. This vision has been greatly influenced by the Maori, the indigenous people of New Zealand. As we spent time with a particular Maori community, we learned about how this subtribe centered its social life around the community center, or *marae*. The *marae*, and the associated land, connected the community members with their ancestors (the past) and their descendents (the future).

This was the concrete space in and through which community life was experienced, and where individuals developed in the context of lives of rich connectedness with others. But the interdependence of the Maori community clearly extended to the land and the waters that had provided them life. Members of particular communities saw themselves as the caretakers of the land within their visual reach—an estuary and adjacent land along the coast that was bounded by ridges on three sides. As efforts by the larger community were carried out to restore tracks of land to native forests, allowing the native, endangered birds to flourish, the Maori saw this as increasing their *mana*—their prestige, character, and honor—because it represented their fulfillment of their caretaking role. And as the New Zealand government and European population attempts to redress wrongs done to the Maori, they not only restore human relationships among peoples but also restore the native bush. The land and its health cannot be separated from the emotional and cultural health of the Maori themselves, and their sense of personhood that is attached to this particular place.

This description of the Maori illustrates the concept of place in the field of geography. While our healthy development and our capacity to love is grounded in an early attachment to important figures in our lives, this attachment and capacity to love is also tied to the places associated with those early memories.[3] Historian Christopher Lasch claimed that allegiance to the "world" is ineffective because it stretches our capacity for loyalty too thin.[4] In reality, we love particular people in particular places. And mature and psychological well-being is developed and maintained through being grounded in particular communities and places.

A lack of secure attachment early in one's life increases the chances that an individual will relate to others only to the "degree that the other meets some immediate need."[5] I would argue by extension that the lack of attachment of individuals to places that embody expressions of the hu-

3. Horner, *Being and Loving*, 42.

4. Lasch, *The True and Only Heaven*, 36.

5. Horner, *Being and Loving*, 45.

man community and the natural world leads to an inability to love nature and places. Such unattached individuals might typically hold a utilitarian view of the natural environment. Another expression of insecure attachment can also be found in places where appropriate boundaries within the community are lacking. Consider a rural community I recently visited. By measures of volunteer organizational membership, the town was doing well. But a closer look revealed high levels of alcoholism, sexual abuse, and an inability of their young people to survive outside the social circle. Associational membership was an end unto itself, and individuals, unable to define their personhood, could not venture out.

Nature-Society Wholeness

The experience of wholeness that comes from a meaningful and healthy relationship among people, and nature is not confined to indigenous peoples. I once had an Iowa farmer tell me that he had noticed that the birds disappeared during the farm depression of the 1980s. The groaning of humanity, quite literally, had somehow affected the earth.[6] I initially assumed that he was referring to the land-use pattern of the 1980s, created when farmers plowed up the fencerows, leaving no room for wildlife. But the farmer was instead referring to something much deeper. The physical and ecological processes that shaped the landscape somehow connected at some deep level to the moral and psychological life of human society.[7] This web of relationship is expressed in the struggles for wholeness as described by the Apostle Paul, for whom our wholeness as a human community is intertwined with the wholeness and connection we have with the rest of the creation (Rom 8:18–23).

Concrete Spirituality and Ethical Systems

Any vision of nature-culture wholeness is lived out in a particular ecological place. Just as psychological well-being is not developed out of universalistic attachments to humanity, so our full embodiment of our personhood with the natural environment also must be fully embodied in the particulars of a concrete place. After my undergraduate degree, I served with the

6. Curry, "Community Worldview and Rural Systems," 701.
7. Curry-Roper, "Embeddedness in Place," 218.

Mennonite Central Committee (MCC), a volunteer organization. MCC sent me to Southern Louisiana, along the Gulf Coast, to work with the Houma tribe of Native Americans. My assignment was to work with the tribe in establishing a link between their present selves and the historical Houma tribe in order to aid them in their efforts to gain tribal status from the federal government. Through the process of this research I first encountered a concrete expression of the real connection between people and the land or natural environment.

While I was collecting ethnographic material, an elderly Houma woman told me about the "woodsmen," dangerous creatures who lived and ate in trees. When she was young, in one instance, the men had gone hunting when the woodsmen came. The presence of the woodsmen was evident to the women from their horrible smell. In response, the women lit tobacco to keep the woodsmen away.[8] When I asked the Houma woman whether the woodsmen still existed, she gave me a puzzled look. She simply said that the forest had disappeared. She was reflecting the reality around us. The cypress forest had died through the process of building channels for the movement of oil rigs, leaving no habitat for the woodsmen. As the environment changed, mythology and spirituality changed as well.[9] Life is lived as a whole in the context of both culture and nature in particular places.

In another example, anthropologist Keith Basso describes how the Western Apache's ethical system, shaping relationships among members of the tribe, was concretely tied to places through which and natural features near which tribal members walked regularly.[10] He learned that stories were associated with the names of these places. A place-name then became a vehicle for moral teaching. The path to wisdom involved knowing the places, the stories, and their meanings, as well as walking through that space. The moral system that shaped the culture and ensured the health of the human community through the maintenance of healthy relationships within the tribe and between parents and children was grounded in the physical features of their landscape. To remove the Western Apache from their environment would be to undermine the whole fabric of the relationships that maintained a healthy sense of personhood. The aspects of our lives that enable our healthy development—spirituality, appropriate social boundaries, secure attachment—are tied to concrete places and learned in concrete contexts.

8. Curry, "Environmental Care."
9. Ibid.
10. Basso, *Wisdom Sits in Place.*

Knowing and Being Known

To be whole and fully formed people, we must have the ability to connect and bond, not only to other persons, but to the places we encounter. We must be able to know places. In graduate school I took a five-week archeology field course on the bluff above the Minnesota River, excavating a Native American village and an adjacent fur-trading post. After digging test pits to locate the village, and spending several weeks shoveling and sifting, several of us set off over lunch to search for the river. We proceeded to get lost but did find the river, the rapids, an old Swedish farmstead, the slough, and the cane breaks. By midafternoon we had found our way back to our excavation site. Several days later, our professor asked us, the explorers, to find the site of the fur-trading post. The three of us immediately walked to a spot about a quarter mile away through the brush and dug just one test pit and found it. How did we know? To this day I can't tell you. All I can tell you is that we had encountered a place. We knew the blue heron in the slough, the turtle on the rock each morning when we passed, the large glacial erratic—the land itself.[11]

This kind of knowing contrasts with knowing in the academic world where I spend quite a bit of time. In higher education we work at challenging students to see issues in a framework that goes beyond the limitations of the parochial or locally based experiences: college is meant to be a broadening experience. Professors are supposed to belong to the world of ideas rather than to the world of places.[12] But I have come to believe that becoming a healthy individual is linked to the deepening of our attachment to place. When we deepen our understanding, commitment, and attachment to the places where we live, we gain a greater understanding of ourselves through paying attention to the intricacies of our place and our responsibilities.

Out of a growing appreciation for my growth as a person through my encounters with places, I helped develop a program at Calvin College called CEAP (Calvin Environmental Assessment Program). The goal of the program was to help students develop the skill of learning to know a place. We live in a mobile world. Yet, in order to be fully human, we need to develop attachments to places and environments in which we live. CEAP attempts to develop the skills of observation, personal engagement, and

11. Curry, "Environmental Care."
12. Zencey, "The Rootless Professors."

care so that students can draw on them when they inhabit other places throughout their lives. We believe that if students learn to bond with their surroundings as young adults, we will increase their capacity to love other places in the future.

Christian Faith and Place

Attachment to community and place, and a theology that values the earth as God's creation are closely connected. In a study on the environmental perspectives of seminarians at four institutions, I found one group of seminarians who strongly identified attachment to a physical environment and to places as idolatry. These same seminary students could not conceive of the earth and the natural world as having any meaning to God other than as a stage on which God's salvation story for individual humans was played out. In contrast, a second group of seminarians drew on other theological traditions that valued the earth as God's good work and connected a love for the earth to loving and committing themselves to their neighbors and the places where they live.[13] These seminarians valued the multiplicity of attachments as worthy of God's concern and their focus.

The responses of these seminarians reflect recent growth in the theological expressions that take seriously our healthy need for attachment to place. While traditional theological reflection on what it means to be made in the image of God has centered on traits of individual humans, such as rational thought, the social Trinitarian school of theology identifies being made in the image of God with being created for relationship. And in this relatedness, nature is not a neutral backdrop, but rather God, humanity, and nature are inextricably bound up with one another.[14]

Theologian Colin Gunton, coming out of this theological tradition, goes so far as to say that it is wrong to abstract humans from their social context, but it is also wrong to abstract the environment from its inhabitants. He argues that such abstraction empties the world of its personal meaning because humans have a deep desire to be connected to each other and to the earth.[15] I would go even further and say that we fail to become fully actualized and healthy individuals without this attachment to the natural world and to the communities that inhabit it. Social Trinitarian theology broadens and deep-

13. Curry and Groenendyk, "Place and Nature Seen through the Eyes of Faith."

14. Hall, "The Spirituality of the Covenant"; and Hall, *Imagining God*, 124.

15. Gunton, *The One, the Three, and the Many*, 16.

ens the meaning of *shalom*—to be at peace with God, with other people, and with the creation—the webbing together of God, humans, and all creation in justice, fulfillment, and delight. This is what God wishes for us—health and flourishing in real places, not in the abstract. We must proclaim the intrinsic worth and value of being committed to a place and its necessity in our spiritual and psychological health.

What Gets in the Way?

What gets in the way of our reaching for this holistic sense of personhood with strong connections to others, to our communities, and to the ecological places where we live? If this is such an incredibly strong vision of health, why do we not recognize it?

Autonomous Individualism

Perhaps the strongest impediment to our being able to recognize the wholeness and health that comes from a rich and variable complex of attachments is the dominant Western view of humans. This view assumes that we reach full and healthy personhood when we become autonomous individuals, unattached to and disconnected from the social and environmental context. Societal structures assume that aloneness is the fundamental reality of humans. For example, government is seen as having the role of mediating between only individuals. The rights or needs of nature and community—something larger than the individual—is outside our legal and societal imagination. The government, or other entities that provide structures that mediate between humans and nature, and that shape our relationships, are unable to incorporate easily into their framework variables such as community attachment, community vitality and richness, and environmental fit. Such entities see the world as a made up of autonomous individuals because it is so difficult to give concreteness or to commodify the elements that hold the world together like attachments, relationships, and trust. These elements are the aspects of healthy lives between people, and between people and nature. This *betweenness*, so essential for our individual healthy development and the healthy development of communities and nature, remains elusive and unaccounted for in our decision making.

A comparison between two agricultural systems, systems that create de facto boundaries between people, and between people and nature, can illustrate this problem. Industrial corporate hog-production systems make farmers into contractors with multinational corporations. These farmers are given standardized plans for buildings and the production processes. Hogs are then produced in places like North Carolina, with shipments of corn from the Midwest, on a soil base that can neither absorb the manure being produced nor grow the corn needed for the hogs. Such systems are now found in other parts of the country and world, transplanted into very different environments with no further adaptation to local circumstances.[16] These systems are unattached to nature and to local circumstances. Such systems undermine human attachments as well. Farmers with corporate contracts no longer buy supplies from local suppliers. In an interview with such a farmer, I asked him about the price of feed and the price of hogs, but he knew neither. He raised the pigs with feed provided by the corporation and delivered the pigs to the corporation when they grew to the specified size. Animal-rights advocates often miss at least one fundamental issue of such agricultural systems: the farmers' loss of connection to the community and environment within which they live.[17]

In contrast to this industrialized form of hog farming, another system which is just as efficient is the Swedish hooped system. Farmers construct small hooped shelters where manure and straw compost naturally to provide heat without creating a problem with smells in the farm neighborhood, and without polluting water. Hogs are arranged so that they mimic the behavior of hogs in the wild. Because of the smaller size and the safety of the operation, children can be involved in this hog system. Both the marketing of the hogs and the purchase of materials remains embedded in the local community. Attachments to nature, to the local community, and among the family are enhanced through the production system. Attentiveness and knowing others (the animals, and nature) are enhanced through the management of the hooped system as well.

While these two systems are equal in efficiency, society cannot account for the additional benefits of the hooped system. The trust and connections among different aspects of society and the natural world that are maintained and enhanced through the hooped system remain outside of what is easily quantifiable. Yet, attachment and relational aspects of reality are essential for health and well-being.

16. Curry, "Care Theory and 'Caring' Systems of Agriculture."
17. Ibid.

Demoting the Knowledge That Comes from Attachment

A second factor that keeps us from capturing the vision of wholeness explicit in being attached to others and to places is our view of knowledge. The Western view of knowledge requires it to have the objectivity of distance.[18] If we are attached to a place or natural setting, then we are presumed to be biased, or our knowledge of the place is thought to be of less value than an objective or distant perspective. The local or particular then is demoted as emotion and is not looked to for the generation of knowledge. This viewpoint is in great contrast to attachment theory, which finds that our capacity for healthy relationships and our ability to love—both central to being human—arise out of particular relationships and emotional connection.

Why should this knowledge, grounded in attachment and relationship, be included alongside the more distanced, objective knowledge? I did research on the development of a marine reserve on Great Barrier Island in New Zealand. The community experienced a great deal of conflict between locals and the Department of Conservation (DOC). Local people continually said to me of the DOC and their scientific studies, "They never ask us! I've sat here every day for forty years observing the estuary and the brown teal ducks, and ecologists come in and do a one month study, demand I change some type of activity, without ever asking me what I've observed, and then leave."[19] In this case, local knowledge may have had information to contribute to the development of that one objective, scientific study, that was limited in time and space. The involvement of local people, and their observations, in a sense, were also needed as a monitoring system. And, of course, if the goal of the scientific study was environmental health, this goal could not be achieved without its being embedded in the local community. In the case of Great Barrier Island, consensus at the local level was the only means of policing any marine reserve. Nobody else could protect from nighttime poaching the area that extended seaward for twelve miles from the coastline. Commitment to the place and people was essential for an effective management system. Community and nature together form a whole in a place.

I would go one step further, however. Through a rich set of attachments to a setting, we gain knowledge that otherwise would not be accessible to us. We transcend the reality of a narrow set of causes and effects and acquire a wisdom that allows us to know the impact of the interrelationships. This

18. Tronto, *Moral Boundaries.*

19. Curry, "The Nature-Culture Boundary and Oceans' Policy," 61.

type of wisdom is an irreducible component of any relationship to place. New ways of thinking arise as together we approach the natural world in the manner of a conversation.[20] It is a form of growth that emulates the growth of a child as they gain independence from a parent, growing into a dialogue among equals. The higher standard becomes, not our control of nature, but the discovery of a relational process and ways of living that enhance this process, the land, and human community at the scale at which we form relationships.[21]

Models with Essential Elements

In recent years I have become fascinated and encouraged by the growing local-food movement as a response, I believe, to a greater desire for wholeness. In my own place, this finds expression in the establishment of the West Michigan Cooperative. This cooperative allows local consumers to order products online from individual local farmers. The orders are then delivered to a warehouse once a month where individuals pick up their order from the local farmers. Consumers sense the local rhythms of the seasons through what is available, and enjoy volunteering on the delivery day and meeting others from the community.

My region also has seen a growth in the network of community supported agriculture programs (CSAs) as an addition to the mix of growing connections between people and place. By buying shares in a farm, local people become attentive to the risks and seasons. Members share recipes that help them creatively use the produce of the week, or even help identify the vegetables in their basket!

Farmers' markets are also increasing as individuals enjoy both the fresh produce and connection with local farmers, and also the pleasure of greeting friends and colleagues on a Saturday morning in a crowded marketplace. The experience is one of attachment and belonging to both a community and a natural environment.

The local-food movement is but one example of communities trying to reestablish something of what has been lost—the relational aspect of life, including the relation to the natural environment. These movements across many places and situations share commonalities. They all involve community initiatives and empowerment. Those involved in these movements also

20. Berry, *What Are People For?*, 208–9.

21. Jackson, *Altars of Unhewn Stone*, 10, 158.

tend to see the world as a set of relationships and attachments rather than as single-interest groups. Thus it is about building trust and relationships among people who inhabit a geographic space rather than having negotiations among larger national economic sectors. These movements reflect different assumptions about the nature of reality. Their approach starts with the assumption that humans are *fundamentally relational*. Thus these local initiatives involve judging options based on whether particular approaches enhance the relational aspect of reality or not. They start with the assumption that attachment to place is good and necessary for our health and well being. And finally, those involved in these movements assume that we are whole people, embodying the rational and emotional in ourselves. Aspects of ourselves cannot be disassociated from the rest of us or from concrete, real places. In these movements, including the local-food movement, our experiences of wholeness become the goalpost toward which to work. As Nel Noddings says, we must build on the best picture of ourselves caring and being cared for.[22] This picture of our best selves can only take place within the context of places where the full range of relationships and attachments, from human relations alone to relationships between humans and the natural environment, can be nurtured and flourish in their full complexity.

My Place

More than a decade ago my family and I moved to Grand Rapids. In the search for a house I kept going back to one particular neighborhood. What drew me there? Perhaps something in the built environment—sidewalks or the small neighborhood shopping center—reflected something appealing. Or was it the number of children playing on the sidewalks while parents conversed? As we unpacked and moved into our newly purchased home, multiple neighbors brought food, and one family took my children to play at their home. All the while, these neighbors walked across each others' backyards, unhindered by fences and other obstructions. I knew we had made the right choice. What leads to an urban neighborhood like this one? I speculate that the habits of living embedded in a place—the sense of place—that developed during a time when the neighborhood was more homogeneous have been passed on to the new families, who now come from a variety of ethnic and racial backgrounds. Places continue to develop and come into being through a variety of means.

22. Noddings, *Caring*, 80.

Recently, as I contemplated all these issues, I sat in a coffee shop in my neighborhood shopping center, a district that everyone has worked hard to maintain. The hardware store, against all odds, rebuilt after a fire, and just this fall a new vegetable-and-fruit market opened after a three-years' gap since the closure of the previous grocery store. The new store has much more local produce. The coffee shop, library, and ice cream shop are busy. And recently some of the local churches have joined to form the Stewards of Plaster Creek, a group that is moving the faith community toward action in restoring the creek that travels through this part of the city, providing habitat for everything from wild turkeys to salmon. Through greater attention to our impact on the community of the watershed, we try to work to bring *shalom* in the place where we live.

We are attempting to form spiritual disciplines, or habits of life, that help us know our piece of the earth. I believe my neighbors and I are moving closer to a fully integrated life—into *shalom*—when we experience the joy of the neighborhood children who walk to the Tuesday evening book reading at the ice cream shop, and the excitement of locals who stop to tell us they have seen the wild turkeys on their walk. Through experiencing these things with our children, we increase their ability to love. I experience *shalom* every time I walk to the hardware store with parts from my bathroom shower in my hand, and have the owners hand me replacement pieces *and* tell me how to put the parts all back together. I don't experience that sense of wholeness because my shower will now work, but rather because I am part of a web of relationships within a city where we share a mutual attachment to a place and work together for the health and well-being of all its members—the wild turkeys, the children, the local business district, and our creek. And as a small part of those caring relationships, my shower gets fixed.

Conclusion

CHRISTIAN E. EARLY AND ANNMARIE L. EARLY

THE HUMAN STORY CAN be told in many ways. The science of attachment theory and the faith statement of Christian theology share the conviction that at its deepest, truest, and most basic, the human story is a love story. Attachment theory is really a theory of love; the gospel is really a story of love.[1] The rich expanse of human lived experience can only be fully acknowledged when our sense-making theories and stories are big enough to hold the existential highs of connection and the heartbreaking lows of betrayal, trauma, and loss. Anabaptists would want to go on and claim that the best way to tell that story is to sing it together, and they would not be alone.[2] Poets, thinkers, and mystics of all traditions have agreed that the richness of what makes life meaningful finds fullest articulation in song—and here we come back, we always come back, to the felt resonance of love.[3]

The Christian Scriptures are no exception. While they can (and have) been read in many ways—ways that serve the political purpose of privileging one race, gender, ethnicity, or sexual orientation over another—they are best read as a love story: the love of God is like the love of a mother and a father, who would give up their own lives for the life of their child. But the

1. This is of course not an uncontested claim, especially among Christians. But those who seek to fold the life and death of Jesus of Nazareth into the logic of temple sacrifice grounded in an image of God whose only notion of justice is punishment overlook the deep tension in the Gospels between Jesus and the temple: Jesus forgave people freely (thus triggering the plot to kill him), disrupted temple life upon entering Jerusalem by overturning tables, and foretold the temple's destruction. The conflict is not simply about the practical problem of finding a perfect sacrifice—as if goats and pigeons are just not good enough for God's high standards. Rather, the conflict is theological, which is to say that it is about what God is like, and how one goes about repairing relationship with God.

2. See *Sing the Story I* and *II*. Harrisonburg, VA: Faith and Life Resources. 2007.

3. It is no accident that most, if not all, songs are love songs in one way or another.

Scriptures are an honest love story, as all good love stories must be, and so the Bible vividly demonstrates the power of connection and disconnection in the lived experience of the characters represented in the narratives. The on-the-ground realism of the stories rings true to our own lives. Truthfulness allows attachment theory, the biblical story, and the lived traditions of our faith communities to make contact and give voice to healing and hope in a broken world.

Theology and Science: Where the Conversation Is Moving

The early Anabaptists found a way to make safe community in a world that persecuted them. At their best they became a home to the world, and at their worst they became sealed off to outsiders and to emotions—to the strangers outside and to the (sometimes even more dangerous) strangers inside.

A Christian theology of our inner life has, almost like everything else, traditionally taken its cue from Augustine. The problem with human beings, so he would argue, is that left to our own devices we naturally love what is bad for us (evil, really, when you get right down to it). The antidote was true religion. Religion, for Augustine, did not mean what we now mean in the sense that "there are many religions in the world." Instead, it meant something like committed and faithful practice of the Christian tradition, which slowly trained a human being to love that which is genuinely good. A mark of love is that it does not seek to possess and consume, but allows something to be by receiving it as a gift. The disciple submitted to a rigorously patterned training (the yoke of Christ) until the external Word had become sufficiently internalized and the cursed condition of loving what one ought not love was overcome—except that it could never completely be overcome while the disciple was still in the body.[4]

---

4. An Augustinian analysis is not useless; it just is more descriptive of the adult pathological narcissist—or, writ large, the colonializing empire, see his *City of God*—who sees everything as an extension of self and consequently loves power or profit more than people, animals, and our shared earth. For Augustine, that pathological narcissism was evident in babies from the day they were born: they want things that are actually bad for them, they force their will on everyone around them, and they jealously refuse to share the gifts they have been given. Unlike Augustine, Anabaptists believed in the innocence of children, and partly for this reason (and also to evade being written into the public church registry) they did not practice infant baptism. While all of us to some extent have the potential to become pathological narcissists, the evidence seems clear that they are created through a set of very specific circumstances.

As powerful and important as this theological psychology has been and still is, it seems worth stating that Christian theology need not follow in the footsteps of Augustine. This is good news for those of us who work at integrating theology and science because part of the tension between theology and psychology comes in large part because Augustinian theology cannot very easily take on board Freudian or Lacanian psychology without widespread tension in the web of belief.[5] At any rate, constructing a new theological account of the inner life seems to us to be compellingly and urgently worthwhile. With its understanding of human beings as social animals born to bond, we think that attachment theory would be a good place for a new conversation to start between theology and science, because the resonance between them is so clear. Attachment theory, for example, provides a powerful way to understand the deeply embodied and lived practices of a community rich in service.

Accessibility and responsiveness—the implicit sense that I can reach you and that you will respond—is the nutritious soil out of which secure attachment grows. Being there in practical ways during times of desperate need anchor us in bonds deeper than shared conviction or creed. The power of bonds built during moments of need are enduring, and we remember vividly years later those moments when we felt cared for, as if they happened yesterday. The tangible act of provision and the implicit significance of *being there* support the importance of service acts by people in organizations such as Mennonite Central Committee and Mennonite Disaster Service.[6] What better witness to the world of a God who loves than the empathic response to need?

The Extended Self and an Invitation to Belong

The most important point of serendipitous resonance between the authors is their shared call to redefine the sense of self:

- Dan Siegel argues that in order to address the pressing problems of today, we have to get rid of the idea that the self ends with the skin. He

5. This long-standing tension points to the possibility that Augustinianism and Freudianism or Lacanianism may be incommensurate, which would explain the disease theologians have had with respect to psychology. At an institutional level, very few seminaries intentionally work at integrating theology and psychology. Fuller Seminary is a notable exception.

6. Online: www.mcc.org and www.mds.mennonite.net/.

defines integration, which is at the center of his thinking, as linking differentiated parts, and imagines a river of integration flowing between the banks of chaos and rigidity. For him, integration is health.

- Jim Coan's research highlights that the brain does not make a hard distinction between your being under threat and my being under threat. From the brain's perspective, I am you, and you are me.

- Sue Johnson provides the image of Argentinian tango in which dancers can feel the next step as their bodies coordinate fluid movements as one. It is a neural duet. It is a dance of love.

- John Paul Lederach tells the story of Balu, whose courage and song transformed enemies into friends, and he explores the metaphor of the singing bowl, whose sound can be felt before it can be heard, and whose bubbling waters heal.

- Nancey Murphy shows that the notion of an extended self fits much better with biblical conceptions of what it means to be human and also makes much better sense of otherwise puzzling passages. One thinks here, for example, of Jesus' use of the image of the vine and the branches in the Gospel of John (chapter 15) and the language of dwelling and abiding. One also thinks of Paul's use of the image of the body and his claim that we share in each other's suffering and joy (1 Cor 12).

- Janel Curry insists that we are so shaped by place that the boundaries of our sense of self and our environment not only are fuzzy but overlap and are interconnected. We cannot understand who we are without telling that story too.[7]

Attachment theory offers a starting place to engage more deeply what it means to be human and to expand our sense of self. The basic processes active in creating a secure connection move to the music of processes implicit

---

7. See here David James Duncan, *My Story as Told by Water*. In an intriguing discussion of the modern and Newtonian idea that matter is inert—an idea that was challenged by Joseph Priestly and theological nonconformists—Stephen Toulmin, says that human actions were not viewed as influencing the workings of nature significantly in part because the natural world was not yet understood as an ecological network of biological systems. Instead, nature was understood as a "background or state setting on which the human drama was being played out . . . [and] presumably this drama would run its course without changing the basic makeup of nature" (Toulmin, *Cosmopolis*, 109). If matter is not understood as inert but as active, then it plays a part in the drama and isn't merely its setting.

and experienced bodily. As many of the authors have noted, metaphors of music—resonance, vibration, and inner movement—best describe this place of fluid contact and connection. In this space, action is more felt than seen. It is the space of limbic, bottom-up *feeling felt,* of lived experience that communicates presence, the emotional engagement and contact of secure connection. It is exactly here that advances in neuroscience and findings from attachment theory are most useful to those who wish to learn the gentle art of healing. It requires song leaders who allow emotional melodies to play, who recognize the importance of the emotional space of the other in our overall well-being through the shared regulation of our emotions.

This may be as good a place as any to state once and for all that secure attachment is not enmeshment. Empathic attunement and availability are hard-wired necessities for healthy human functioning; the evidence here is overwhelming and unequivocal. This is not to deny that enmeshment names an actual reality; it sure does! Small communities—and Mennonite communities are not immune—often have this quality. Rather, properly understood, what we have been taught to call enmeshment is the result of an insecure form of connection that constricts and binds because it is born of anxiety, shame, or the need to control.

The key here is to understand the deep, powerful, and enduring attachment dynamics that underlie the lack of individuation and that keep that lack in place. In this light, enmeshment can be located squarely in the familiar landscape of insecure attachment, and it is often evident in places where physical needs are met, but where the deeper implicit communication and contact of emotional attunement are absent. One must have healthy connection in order to differentiate. Safe-haven security is a prerequisite for secure-base exploration (i.e., differentiation). One cannot, at least not without great difficulty, explore with abandon without the felt knowing that someone is there when we return. Living in the heart and mind of another helps us to venture out, to become our own person, and to carry on.[8]

The melodies of secure attachment inevitably come with their awkward edges of misattunement. *Being there when needed,* which is the crucial ingredient for secure connection, is part of the human rhythm of rupture and repair. The inner sense of relational safety is built on the not-always-getting-it-right of life where mistakes are acknowledged and connections are repaired. The same dance of misattunement and restored resonance witnessed between mother and child is also necessary for strong communal

8. See Bowlby, *A Secure Base*; and Mikulincer and Shaver, *Attachment in Adulthood.*

living. When we move past signals of danger, and experience greater safety within community, we are better able to engage honest conversation. We feel safe enough to invite truth telling without shame, to acknowledge our own shortcomings more openly, to ask for forgiveness, and to appreciate authentic *moments of meeting* that evoke delight.[9] The community quilt knit and reknit from this fabric is stronger because of repaired ruptures, and its resilience releases us for engagement with the stranger within and among us. It is from this place that invitation to join is compelling as the *feeling felt* of being known becomes a safe space for true hospitality, a healing home to a traumatized world.

From Darwin to Jesus and Back Again

How we ought to live (ethics) cannot be made to be independent of who we are biologically.[10] The problem has been, however, that the picture we all too often received from biology was that (our) nature was essentially competitive and selfish. As we pointed out in the introduction, Darwin himself came to see that this picture of animal behavior was at best too narrow and very likely false. Close study of *actual* animal behavior (ethology) revealed—and continues to reveal—a much richer story.[11]

A more recent example of a similar shift can be found in the writings of Frans de Waal. Reflecting on a previous book that he wrote on chimpanzee power politics and aggression in a zoo, which at the time had struck him as essentially Machiavellian (the power politics, not the zoo, although with all that we now know about top-down causation, one has to wonder), de Waal says that he was surprised to notice "a great need in the apes to maintain social relationships, make up after fights, and reassure distressed parties, which got me thinking about empathy and cooperation."[12] De Waal, like Darwin before him, began to notice the rich inner and emotional life of the apes he was studying—and this careful ethology has made all the difference

9. Stern, *The Present Moment in Psychotherapy and Everyday Life.*

10. See MacIntyre, *Dependent Rational Animals* and Churchland, *Braintrust.*

11. There is a peculiar way in which theologians, philosophers, and scientists tend to see nothing but the law of competition and selfishness when they look back at the origins and dynamics of humankind. Whether it is original sin, the will to power, or the fitness calculation of a gene (a clever little thing, apparently), the dark picture tends to be the same. Might this be a case of projection?

12. See de Waal, *The Age of Empathy*, 233. The previous book to which he refers is his *Chimpanzee Politics*, which was originally published in 1982.

for his understanding of how to characterize animal *nature* (to use that great blank canvas of a word).[13]

Human beings have, puzzlingly, a great capacity for both good and evil. If we are not essentially selfish and competitive, as some would have it, then how do we explain all the (sometimes incomprehensible and massive) evil and cruelty that we see around us? In *The Science of Evil*, Simon Baron-Cohen argues convincingly that cruelty and evil are the result of a lack or an erosion of empathy.[14] Drawing on Martin Buber's distinction between *I-you* and *I-it*, Baron-Cohen says that "when our empathy is switched off, we are solely in the 'I' mode. In such a state we relate only to things or to people as if they were just things. . . . Treating other people as if they were just objects is one of the worst things you can do to another human being, to ignore their subjectivity, their thoughts and feelings."[15] Empathy erodes, in other words, when we refuse to acknowledge the presence of another human being (or animal or environment) as an invitation to relationship. Given the evidence that we are born to bond, the arrow of refusal points back at ourselves as well: in refusing to acknowledge the invitation to relationship by saying we don't care, we are also refusing to acknowledge who we most basically are, and we disfigure ourselves.

Jesus told the story of the Good Samaritan as an answer to a lawyer's question, "What must I do to inherit eternal life?" (Luke 10:25). We would probably do the text and ourselves a favor by interpreting eternal life qualitatively instead of quantitatively (fullness of life rather than live forever). Read that way, it is a question that speaks to the meaning of life and to whether there is a meaning deeper than survival. In his *Empathic Civilization*, Jeremy Rifkin points out that a growing number of scholars argue that the awe-inspiring and stunning complexity and extension we observe in biological life cannot be explained simply by the drive to survive and reproduce. If it were only about survival, human beings, for example, would have kept their population smaller. Something else must be going on; something deeper must be at work.

13. Here again is the shift that comes from gaining a sense of depth. The difference can be seen in de Waal's books such as *Peacemaking among Primates* (1990), *Good Natured* (1997), *The Age of Empathy* (2010), and most recently *The Primate Mind* (2012).

14. Baron-Cohen, *The Science of Evil*.

15. Ibid., 7–8. See also Buber, *I and Thou*. For Buber, "I–you" names a mode of being and relating in which the other person is an end, whereas "I–It" names a mode of being and relating in which the other person is a means to an end. This is not the only distinction between the two modes, but it is a fundamental one.

Rifkin says:

> If we are by nature an affectionate species that continuously seeks
> to broaden and deepen our relationships and connections to oth-
> ers, in effect to transcend ourselves by participating in more ex-
> pansive communities of meaning, then our increasingly complex
> social structures provide the vehicles for our journey. . . . We do
> so in order to find meaning in belonging to ever richer and deeper
> realms of reality.[16]

A little later he writes:

> We begin to sense the possibility that there may be a purpose after
> all to the human journey: that the deepening sense of selfhood,
> the extension of empathy to broader and more inclusive domains
> of reality and the expansion of human consciousness, is the tran-
> scendent process by which we explore the mystery of existence
> and discover new realms of meaning.[17]

The idea that every innovation is ultimately explained by genetic per-
petuation quite simply begs the question. There is a deeper meaning to life
than mere survival. That need to connect and belong to richer and deeper
realms of reality—to transcend ourselves—is what fuels the scientific (and
we should add here philosophical and theological) quest.[18] At heart, deepening our sense of selfhood and extending empathy to more inclusive do-
mains of reality is a spiritual quest. Do that, says Jesus (referring the lawyer
back to loving God and loving neighbor), and you will live.

Conclusion to the Conclusion:
From Attachment to Christian Community

In a recent article, we coined the term *affect narratives* to help remind us
that paying attention to the inner drama and plot of a community can
reveal key moments of rupture and help identify a path of repair.[19] We
believe that healing comes not merely in telling the content of the story,
but in *how* one tells the story. To tell our story with engaged emotionality,

16. Rifkin, *The Empathic Civilization*, 39–40.

17. Ibid., 40.

18. Ironically, it is often our science, philosophy, and theology that alienate us from
ourselves, our human family, and our world.

19. See Early and Early, "The Neuroscience of Emotion."

not only communicates contact through language, but offers a message that connects to the deeply embedded neurocircuitry of our lived experience. We have offered attachment theory as a perspective that helps us better to understand and articulate key aspects of what it means to be followers of Jesus together: acknowledging the power of specific practices in creating bonds and change events, honoring the lived integration through community, and gaining an appreciation for self-reflective growth. This open stance would allow greater felt experience of emotion and would seek to not silence the pain of mistakes but better understand the effects of rupture and seek the power of repair in healing.

We want to join our voices to the conversation about what it means to be human, offering the wisdom of the Anabaptist tradition of concrete service, actual community, and vision of peace with the powerful advances in affective neuroscience and attachment. They speak of a way of being human that allows us to see our very essence through fresh eyes. Siegel describes a flowing river of integration in which the quality of engagement is characterized by openness and exploration.[20] John sees a river of healing flowing out to all the nations (Rev 22). This is a vision that acknowledges deep human suffering and woundedness. It offers healing to broken lives and relationships, and it nourishes hope for a different tomorrow. It is a light shining in the darkness, orienting us and inviting us to come home. It is a song, and when we sing it, we begin again to find our way as aborigines one and all.

The Anabaptist story is one of community and compassion, a story of persecution and love, and our hope is that it becomes a story infused with play and intersubjective delight. We want the larger world to hear the Anabaptist story in a way that emboldens their next steps and offers images of accompanying relationship along the way. As we move toward health—the integration that creates wholeness in self and society—we need conversations that encourage greater embodiment in both concept and lived experience. And whether spoken from John Bowlby or John the Seer, the need for a safe-haven respite is crucial for healing and a secure-base platform allowing exploration where anything is possible. The Christian call is to serve as Jesus served and to extend an invitation to the outsider to find home with a people attempting to live out his example and call to nonviolence in the conviction that *this* is our true and coming home: the kingdom of God among us, a God whom Jesus taught us to call *Abba*.

20. See Siegel, *Mindsight*.

Bibliography

Ainsworth, Mary D. Salter et al. *Patterns of Attachment: A Psychological Study of the Strange Situation.* Hillsdale, NJ: Erlbaum, 1978.

Armstrong, Karen. *The Case for God.* New York: Anchor, 2010.

Aron, Arthur et al. "Inclusion of Other in the Self Scale and the Structure of Interpersonal Closeness." *Journal of Personality and Social Psychology* 63 (1992) 596–612.

Aron, Arthur et al. "Falling in Love: Prospective Studies of Self-Concept Change." *Journal of Personality & Social Psychology* 69/6 (1995) 1102–12.

Atkinson, Judy. *Trauma Trails, Recreating Song Lines: The Transgenerational Effects of Trauma in Indigenous Australia.* North Melbourne, Australia: Spinifex, 2002.

Augustine, Saint. *City of God.* Translated by Henry Bettenson. London: Penguin, 2003.

———. *Confessions.* Translated by Henry Chadwick. Oxford: Oxford University Press, 1991.

Baron-Cohen, Simon. *The Science of Evil: On Empathy and the Origins of Cruelty.* New York: Basic Books, 2011.

Basso, Keith H. *Wisdom Sits in Place: Landscape and Language among the Western Apache.* Albuquerque: University of New Mexico Press, 1996.

Beckes, Lane, James A. Coen, and Karen Hasselmo. "Familiarity Promotes the Blurring of Self and Other in the Neural Representation of Threat." *Social Cognitive and Affective Neuroscience* 8/6 (2013) 670–77.

Berry, Wendell. *What Are People For? Essays.* San Francisco: North Point, 1990.

Bertalanffy, Ludwig von. *General Systems Theory: Foundations, Development, and Applications.* New York: Braziller, 1968.

Blair, Alexander. "Christian Ambivalence toward the Old Testament: An Investigative Tool in Fundamental Theology." PhD diss., Graduate Theological Union, 1989.

Bowlby, John. *Attachment and Loss.* Vol. 1, *Attachment.* 2nd ed. 3 vols. New York: Basic Books, 1982.

———. *Attachment and Loss.* Vol. 2, *Separation: Anxiety and Anger.* New York: Basic Books, 1976.

———. *Attachment and Loss.* Vol. 3, *Loss: Sadness and Depression.* New York: Basic Books, 1982.

———. *Charles Darwin: A New Life.* New York: Norton, 1991.

———. *A Secure Base: Parent-Child Attachment and Healthy Human Development.* New York: Basic Books, 1988.

Bretherton, I. "The Origins of Attachment Theory: John Bowlby and Mary Ainsworth." *Developmental Psychology* 28 (1992) 759–75.

Brothers, Leslie. *Friday's Footprint: How Society Shapes the Human Mind*. New York: Oxford University Press, 2001.

Buber, Martin. *I and Thou*. Translated by Walter Kaufmann. New York: Scribner, 1970.

Cacciopo, John T., and William Patrick. *Loneliness: Human Nature and the Need for Social Connection*. New York: Norton, 2008.

Carver, Raymond. *A New Path to the Waterfall: Poems*. Introduction by Tess Gallagher. New York: Atlantic Monthly Press, 1989.

Cary, Phillip. *Augustine's Invention of the Inner Self: The Legacy of a Christian Platonist*. Oxford: Oxford University Press, 2000.

Cassidy, Jude, and Phillip R. Shaver, editors. *The Handbook of Attachment: Theory, Research and Clinical Applications*. 2nd ed. New York: Guilford, 2010.

Chatwin, Bruce. *The Songlines*. New York: Viking, 1987.

Coontz, Stephanie. *Marriage, A History: From Obedience to Intimacy or How Love Conquered Marriage*. New York: Viking, 2005.

Curry, Janel M. "Care Theory and 'Caring' Systems of Agriculture." *Agriculture and Human Values* 19 (2002) 119–31.

————. "Community Worldview and Rural Systems: A Study of Five Communities in Iowa." *Annals of the Association of American Geographers* 90 (2000) 693–712.

————. "Environmental Care: A Vision of Community and Land." *Stimulus: The New Zealand Journal of Christian Thought and Practice* 11 (2003) 11–14.

————. "The Nature-Culture Boundary and Oceans' Policy: Great Barrier Island, New Zealand." *The Geographical Review* 97 (2007) 46–66.

Curry, Janel M., and Kathi Groenendyk. "Place and Nature Seen through the Eyes of Faith: Understandings among Male and Female Seminarians." *Worldviews: Environment, Culture, Religion* 10 (2006) 326–54.

Curry-Roper, Janel M. "Embeddedness in Place: Its Role in the Sustainability of a Rural Farm Community in Iowa." *Space and Culture Issue* 4/5 (2000) 204–22.

Dalai Lama. *Beyond Religion: Ethics for a Whole World*. Boston: Houghton Mifflin Harcourt, 2011.

Damásio, Antonio. *Descartes' Error: Emotion, Reason, and the Human Brain*. New York: Avon, 1994.

Darwin, Charles. *The Expression of Emotions in Man and Animals*. London: John Murray, 1872.

————. *On the Origin of Species*. 6th ed. New York: Collier, 1962.

Dawkins, Richard. *The Selfish Gene*. 2nd ed. Oxford: Oxford University Press, 1989.

Domes, Gregor et al. "Oxytocin Improves 'Mind-Reading' in Humans." *Biological Psychiatry* 61/6 (2007) 731–33.

Duncan, David James. *My Story as Told by Water: Confessions, Druidic Rants, Reflections, Bird-Watchings, Fish-Stalkings, Visions, Songs and Prayers Refracting Light, from Living Rivers, in the Age of the Industrial Dark*. San Francisco: Sierra Club Books, 2001.

Eisenberger, Naomi I. et al. "Neural Pathways Link Social Support to Attenuated Neuroendocrine Stress Responses." *NeuroImage* 35 (2007) 1601–2.

————. "Why Rejection Hurts: A Common Neural Alarm System for Physical and Social Pain." *Trends in Cognitive Science* 8 (2004) 294–300.

Early, Christian, and Annmarie Early. "The Neuroscience of Emotion: Attachment Theory and the Practice of Conflict Resolution." *ACResolution* Summer (2011) 9–13.

Feeney, Brooke C. "The Dependency Paradox in Close Relationships: Accepting Dependence Promotes Independence." *Journal of Personality and Social Psychology* 92 (2007) 268–85.

Feyerabend, Paul. *Against Method*. 3rd ed. New York: Verso, 1993.

Galileo, Galilei. *Dialogue Concerning the Two Chief World Systems*. Translated by Stillman Drake. Modern Library Science Series. New York: Modern Library, 2001.

Goleman, Daniel. *Social Intelligence: The New Science of Human Relationships*. New York: Bantam, 2006.

Gottman, John et al. "Predicting Marital Happiness and Stability from Newlywed Interactions." *Journal of Marriage and the Family* 60 (1998) 5–22.

———. "Reply to 'From Basic Research to Interventions'." *Journal of Marriage & Family* 62/1 (2000) 265.

Gottman, John Mordechai. *What Predicts Divorce?: The Relationship between Marital Processes and Marital Outcomes*. New York: Psychology Press, 1994.

Gunton, Colin E. *The One, the Three and the Many: God, Creation, and the Culture of Modernity*. Cambridge: Cambridge University Press, 1993.

Hall, Douglas John. *Imaging God: Dominion as Stewardship*. 1986. Reprinted, Eugene, OR: Wipf & Stock, 2004.

———. "The Spirituality of the Covenant: Imaging God, Stewarding Earth." *Perspectives* December (1988) 11–14.

Hawkley, Louise C., and John T. Cacciopo. "Loneliness Matters: A Theoretical and Empirical Review of Consequences and Mechanisms." *Annals of Behavioral Medicine* 40/2 (2010) 218–27.

Hofer, Myron A. "Hidden Regulators in Attachment, Separation, and Loss." *Monographs of the Society for Research in Child Development* 59/2–3 (1994) 192–207.

Horner, Althea J. *Being and Loving*. Northvale, NJ: Aronson, 1986.

House, James S. et al. "Social Relationships and Health." *Science* 241 (1988) 540–45.

Huston, Caughlin et al. "The Connubial Crucible." *Journal of Personality and Social Psychology* 80/2 (2001) 237–52.

Iacoboni, Marco. *Mirroring People: The Science of Empathy and How We Connect to Others*. New York: Picador, 2009.

Jackson, Wes. *Altars of Unhewn Stone: Science and the Earth*. San Francisco: North Point Press, 1987.

Johnson, Aubrey R. *The One and the Many in the Israelite Conception of God*. 1961. Reprinted, Eugene, OR: Wipf & Stock, 2006.

Johnson, Susan M. *Hold Me Tight: Seven Conversations for a Lifetime of Love*. New York: Little, Brown, 2008.

———. *The Practice of Emotionally Focused Couple Therapy: Creating Connection*. New York: Routledge, 2004.

Jordan, Martin. "Nature and Self—An Ambivalent Attachment?" *Ecopsychology* 1 (2009) 26–31.

Karen, Robert. *Becoming Attached: First Relationships and How They Shape Our Capacity to Love*. New York: Oxford University Press, 1994.

Kauffman, Stuart A. *Reinventing the Sacred: A New View of Science, Reason, and Religion*. New York: Basic Books, 2008.

Kerr, Fergus. *Theology after Wittgenstein*. 2nd ed. London: SPCK, 1997.

Keysers, Christian. *The Empathic Brain: How the Discovery of Mirror Neurons Changes Our Understanding of Human Nature*. Lexington, KY: Social Brain Press, 2011.

Keysers, Christian, and Valeria Gazzola, "Towards a Unifying Neural Theory of Social Cognition." *Progress in Brain Research* 156 (2006) 379–400.

Kling, A. S., and Leslie Brothers. "The Amygdala and Social Behavior." In *The Amygdala: Neurobiological Aspects of Emotion, Memory, and Mental Dysfunction*, edited by John P. Aggleton, 353–77. New York: Wiley-Liss, 1992.

Kornfield, Jack. *A Path with Heart: A Guide through the Perils and Promises of Spiritual Life.* New York: Bantam, 1993.

Lasch, Christopher. *The True and Only Heaven: Progress and Its Critics.* New York: Norton, 1991.

Lash, Nicholas. *Easter in Ordinary: Reflections on Human Experience and the Knowledge of God.* The Richard Lectures for 1986, University of Virginia. Charlottesville: University Press of Virginia, 1988.

Lederach, John Paul, and Angela J. Lederach. *When Blood and Bones Cry Out: Journeys through the Soundscape of Healing and Reconciliation.* New York: Oxford University Press, 2011.

LeDoux, Joseph. *The Synaptic Self: How Our Brains Become Who We Are.* New York: Viking, 2003.

Leopold, Aldo. *A Sand County Almanac.* New York: Oxford University Press, 1949.

Lewis, Thomas et al. *A General Theory of Love.* New York: Vintage, 2000.

Lyte, Henry Francis. *Remains of Henry Francis Lyte.* 1850.

MacIntyre, Alasdair. *Dependent Rational Animals: Why Human Beings Need the Virtues.* Chicago: Open Court, 1999.

Magee, Bryan. *Confessions of a Philosopher: A Personal Journey through Western Philosophy from Plato to Popper.* New York: Modern Library, 1999.

Malina, Bruce J. *The New Testament World: Insights from Cultural Anthropology.* 3rd ed. Louisville: Westminster John Knox, 2001.

McGilchrist, Iain. *The Master and His Emissary: The Divided Brain and the Making of the Western World.* New Haven: Yale University Press, 2012.

Mackay, Susan K. "Nurturance: A Neglected Dimension in Family Therapy with Adolescents." *Journal of Marital and Family Therapy* 22 (1996) 489–508.

Main Mary et al. "Studying Difference in Language Usage in Recounting Attachment History: An Introduction to the AAI." In *Clinical Applications of the Adult Attachment Interview*, edited by Howard Steele and Miriam Steele, 31–68. New York: Guilford, 2008.

Makinen, Judy A., and Susan M. Johnson. "Resolving Attachment Injuries in Couples Using Emotion Focused Therapy: Steps toward Forgiveness and Reconciliation." *Journal of Consulting and Clinical Psychology* 74/6 (2006) 1055–64.

Midgley, Mary. "The Soul's Successors: Philosophy and the 'Body.'" In *Religion and the Body*, edited by Sarah Coakley, 53–68. Cambridge Studies in Religious Traditions 8. Cambridge: Cambridge University Press 1997.

Mikulincer, Mario, and Phillip R. Shaver, editors. *Attachment in Adulthood: Structure, Dynamics, and Change.* New York: Guilford, 2007.

Miller, Roman, and Christian Early. "A Transdisciplinary Exploration of Attachment through Anabaptist Eyes." Unpublished grant proposal.

Teresa, Mother. *Mother Teresa: Come Be My Light; The Private Writings of the "Saint of Calcutta."* Edited by Brian Kolodiejchuk. New York: Doubleday, 2007.

Murphy, Nancey. *Theology in the Age of Scientific Reasoning.* Cornell Studies in the Philosophy of Religion. Ithaca: Cornell University Press, 1990.

—————. *Beyond Liberalism and Fundamentalism: How Modern and Postmodern Philosophy Set the Theological Agenda.* Valley Forge, PA: Trinity, 1996.

Murphy, Nancey, and Warren S. Brown. *Did My Neurons Make Me Do It? Philosophical and Neurobiological Perspectives on Moral Responsibility and Free Will.* Oxford: Oxford University Press, 2009.

Newton, Isaac. *The Principia: Mathematical Principles of Natural Philosophy.* Translated by B. I. Cohen and A. Whitman. Berkeley: University of California Press, 1999.

Noddings, Nel. *Caring: A Feminine Approach to Ethics and Moral Education.* Berkeley: University of California Press, 1984.

Panksepp, Jaak. *Affective Neuroscience: The Foundations of Human and Animal Emotions.* Series in Affective Science. New York: Oxford University Press, 2004.

—————. *The Archaeology of Mind: Neuroevolutionary Origins of Human Emotion.* New York: Norton, 2012.

Porges, Stephen W. *Polyvagal Theory: Neurophysiological Foundations of Emotions, Attachment, Communication,and Self-Regulation.* The Norton Series on Interpersonal Neurobiology. New York: Norton, 2011.

Prigogine, Ilya. *The End of Certainty: Time, Chaos, and the New Laws of Nature.* New York: Free Press, 1997.

Proffitt, Dennis. R. "Embodied Perception and the Economy of Action." *Perspectives on Psychological Science* 1 (2006) 110–22.

Rifkin, Jeremy. *The Empathic Civilization: The Race to Global Consciousness in a World in Crisis.* New York: Tarcher/Penguin, 2009.

Rorty, Richard. *Philosophy and the Mirror of Nature.* Princeton: Princeton University Press, 1980.

Rubin, E. "Figure and Ground." In *Visual Perception: Essential Readings.* Key Readings in Cognition, edited by Steven Yantis, 225–29. Philadelphia: Psychology Press, 2001.

Schnall, Simone et al. "Social Support and the Perception of Geographical Slant." *Journal of Experimental Social Psychology* 44 (2008) 1246–55.

Schore, Allen N. "The Effects of Early Relational Trauma on Right Brain Development, Affect Regulation, and Infant Mental Health." *Infant Mental Health Journal* 22/1–2 (2001) 201–69.

—————. "Right Brain Affect Regulation: An Essential Mechanism of Development, Trauma, Dissociation, and Psychotherapy." In *The Healing Power of Emotion: Affective Neuroscience, Development and Clinical Practice,* edited by Diana Fosha et al., 112–44. The Norton Series on Interpersonal Neurobiology. New York: Norton, 2009.

Schore, Judith R., and Allen N. Schore. "Modern Attachment Theory: The Central Role of Affect Regulation in Development and Treatment." *Clinical Social Work Journal* 36 (2008) 9–20.

Siegel, Daniel J. *The Developing Mind: How Relationships and the Brain Interact to Shape Who We Are.* 2nd ed. New York: Guilford, 2012.

—————. *The Mindful Therapist: A Clinician's Guide to Mindsight and Neural Integration.* The Norton Series on Interpersonal Biology. New York: Norton, 2010.

—————. *Mindsight: The New Science of Personal Transformation.* New York: Bantam, 2010.

Siegel, Daniel J., and Mary Hartzell. *Parenting from the Inside Out.* New York: Tarcher, 2004.

Sing the Story. Harrisonburg, VA: Faith and Life Resources, 2007.

Sroufe, Alan, and Daniel Siegel. "The Verdict Is In: The Case for Attachment Theory." *Psychotherapy Networker* March/April (2010). Online: http://www.psychotherapynetworker.org/magazine/recentissues/1271-the-verdict-is-in/.

Stern, Daniel N. *The Present Moment in Psychotherapy and Everyday Life.* Norton Series on Interpersonal Neurobiology New York: Norton, 2004.

Taylor, Shelley E. et al. "Neural Bases of Moderation of Cortisol Stress Responses by Psychosocial Resources." *Journal of Personality & Social Psychology* 95/1 (2008) 197–211.

Teicher, Martin H. et al. "Childhood Neglect Is Associated with Reduced Corpus Callosum Area" *Biological Psychiatry* 56/2 (2004) 80–85.

Teresa of Avila, Saint. *The Interior Castle.* Translated by E. Allison Peers. Mineola, NY: Dover, 2007.

Thomson, J. Anderson. *Why We Believe in God(s): A Concise Guide to the Science of Faith.* Charlottesville, VA: Pitchstone, 2011.

Toulmin, Stephen. *Cosmopolis: The Hidden Agenda of Modernity.* Chicago: University of Chicago Press, 1992.

Tronick, Edward. *The Neurobehavioral and Socio-Emotional Development of Infants and Children.* The Norton Series on Interpersonal Neurobiology. New York: Norton, 2007.

———, director. *The Still Face Experiment.* Video uploaded November 30, 2009. *Youtube.* www.youtube.com/watch?v=apzXGEbZhto/.

Tronto, Joan C. *Moral Boundaries: A Political Argument for an Ethic of Care.* New York: Routledge, 1994.

Tulving, Endel. *Elements of Episodic Memory.* Oxford Psychology Series 2. Oxford: Clarendon, 1985.

Waal, Frans de. *The Age of Empathy: Nature's Lessons for a Kinder Society.* New York: Three Rivers, 2009.

———. *Chimpanzee Politics: Power and Sex among Apes.* New York: Harper & Row, 1982.

———. *Good Natured: The Origins of Right and Wrong in Humans and Other Animals.* Cambridge: Harvard University Press, 1997.

———. *Our Inner Ape: A Leading Primatologist Explains Why We Are Who We Are.* New York: Riverhead, 2006.

———. *Peacemaking among Primates.* Cambridge: Harvard University Press, 1990.

Waal, Frans de, and Pier Francesco Ferrari. *The Primate Mind: Built to Connect with Other Minds.* Cambridge: Harvard University Press, 2012.

White Jr., Lynn. "The Historical Roots of Our Ecologic Crisis." *Science* March 10 (1967) 1203–7.

Wylie, Mary Sykes, and Lynn Turner. "The Attuned Therapist: Does Attachment Theory Really Matter?" *Psychotherapy Networker Magazine* March/April (2010). Online: http://www.psychotherapynetworker.org/magazine/recentissues/1261-the-attunded-therapist.

Yalom, Marilyn. *The History of the Wife.* New York: HarperPerennial, 2002.

Yoder, John Howard. *Body Politics: Five Practices of the Christian Community before the Watching World.* Harrisonburg, VA: Herald, 2001.

———. *The Politics of Jesus.* 2nd ed. Grand Rapids: Eerdmans, 1994.

Zencey, Eric. "The Rootless Professors." In *Rooted in the Land: Essays on Community and Place*, edited by William Vitek and Wes Jackson, 15–19. New Haven: Yale University Press (1996).

Zhang, Dongyong, and Marcus E. Raichle. "Disease and the Brain's Dark Energy," *Nature Reviews Neurology* 6/1 (2010) 15–28.

Subject Index

Scripture Index